Eat MORE VEGETABLES

Eat MORE VEGETABLES

MAKING THE MOST OF YOUR SEASONAL PRODUCE

TRICIA CORNELL

Minnesota Historical
Society Press

www.mhspress.org

The Minnesota Historical Society Press is a member of the Association of American University Presses.

Manufactured in the United States

10 9 8 7 6 5 4 3 2 1

∞ The paper used in this publication meets the minimum requirements of the American National Standard for Information Sciences—Permanence for Printed Library Materials, ANSI Z39.48–1984.

International Standard Book Number
ISBN: 978-0-87351-852-9 (cloth)

Library of Congress Cataloging-in-Publication Data
Cornell, Tricia.
  Eat more vegetables : making the most of your seasonal produce / Tricia Cornell.
    p. cm.
  Includes index.
  ISBN 978-0-87351-852-9 (cloth : alk. paper)
  1. Cooking (Vegetables) 2. Salads. I. Title.
  TX801.C629 2012
  641.6'5—dc23

                                                        2012003621

Illustrations by Gary Dougherty

For Bruce,
who makes everything possible
and makes it all worthwhile

CONTENTS

Eat MORE VEGETABLES

INTRODUCTION

There was a time when I dreaded Thursdays. Thursday is the day I pick up our CSA share. I stop by a neighbor's driveway with a couple of grocery bags and unpack a big yellow plastic box full of vegetables grown on a farm about sixty miles away.

David Van Eeckhout of Hog's Back Farm in Arkansaw, Wisconsin, packs 170 plastic boxes with somewhere between ten and twenty-five pounds of vegetables every Thursday morning throughout the summer and fall and delivers them to spots in Minneapolis and St. Paul, where people like me—members of his community-supported agriculture (CSA) farm—pick them up. We became Hog's Back members about eight years ago because, as tends to happen, the appearance of a new baby in our lives made my husband and me think hard about what we were putting in our bodies. Local food, free of pesticides, grown by someone we knew and trusted, became more appealing with every bagged-spinach recall and salmonella outbreak. More important, however, we wanted to eat more vegetables, and having those vegetables show up—in all their tempting beauty—every week was how we decided we would accomplish that goal. In June the box holds glistening heads of lettuce, picked that very morning and still miraculously both firm and tender. In July come snap peas and green beans so young and fresh they don't even need cooking. August brings tomatoes—stripy green, scarlet, and purply black—and sugary sweet corn. In September the winter squash, a proud procession of hardy, firm-fleshed, uniquely flavored gourds, starts. October returns us to some of the flavors of spring, with cold frame spinach and broccoli. Our last box in November always offers a feast for the Thanksgiving table, including bright orange sweet potatoes and a long stalk of brussels sprouts. And if I'm lucky there is maple syrup or honey.

But during our first year or two of CSA membership, all I saw on Thursdays was a big box full of obligation. The dread itself was all the more dreadful because our veggie plan was supposed to be such a pleasure. As I put those lovely lettuces in the fridge, I pledged that this week would be different, this week we would use everything and, come hell or high water, we would enjoy it. But the following Wednesday night would come, and there would be limp lettuce or soft zucchini in the crisper, maybe an onion or two sprouting on the counter next to an aging squash with a suspicious soft spot.

When we first signed up for a CSA share, we split it with a friend, knowing that two adults without much time to cook couldn't use a whole box of vegetables in one week. Even so, half a share often overwhelmed us. I threw out more produce than I care to admit and still found myself purchasing out-of-season broccoli or green beans at the grocery store because I wanted them for a recipe or because that was all my daughter was eating at the time. It felt like all our good intentions were rotting away in the crisper.

Then one Saturday morning I picked up a dry-erase marker and opened the refrigerator. "This is the week," I declared. Come Wednesday night, we would have a nearly empty fridge and for the first time I would be glad and grateful to see that yellow box of vegetables. Rarely do such resolutions stick. Nearly eight years later, however, this one has. We still have a dry-erase board in the kitchen, and I still plan meals around our CSA share with a level of obsession that occasionally earns me some mocking from my family. But on Wednesday nights, our fridge is usually (not always) empty.

Around that time I also made a list. I wrote down what my family (there are four of us now) likes to eat for dinner—not what I felt we should eat for dinner, but what we actually enjoy. (Okay, I admit I added in a few things that only I like to eat.) Much of that original list, along with a few fun additions, is here in this book. *Eat More Vegetables* is about how I learned to love Thursdays and to look forward to our CSA share, a story told in recipe form.

Eating meals based on seasonal vegetables, whether they come to you in a big CSA box or you pick them up at the farmers' market or grocery store, takes a bit of planning and a bit of prep work. I'm not here to say it's a snap. But it has become a rewarding part of my family's life. It's become part of the rhythm of our summer. We mark the time by that big yellow box: the time of salads, followed by the time of new potatoes and green beans, followed by the time of zucchini and tomatoes, and then the time of brussels sprouts and squash. I now have memories pegged to particular meals: "Oh, that must have been in July, because I remember we ate outside and had Soupe au Pistou" (p. 107).

Our kids, too, are developing a seasonal memory. My son likes to help wash the many heads of lettuce that arrive in the early boxes. When late June came and I told him that we'd probably washed our last lettuce together for a while, he understood. And now he's looking forward to the fall lettuce that our farmer sows to mature in the cooler weather. My daughter lays immediate claim to the "peas peek out of the pod"—as she christened the snap peas when she was little—knowing that we only get a bag or two of these each summer. My husband likes to survey the table and say contentedly, "Nearly all of this food came from our farmer." Our farmer. We're city folks, so our kids will never say "our farm," but they do think of our CSA farmer as an important part of their lives.

For eight years, David has shared a bit of his family's life and experiences through a personable, smart newsletter that used to come with the CSA box every week and now arrives by e-mail. He provides his "Farmer Complaint Index"—one spectrum running from "Too Hot" to "Too Cold" and another running from "Too Dry" to "Too Wet." He catches us up on the doings about the farm—what equipment has needed repair this week, what pests he's had to knock off the crops, what has gone into the ground, and what has come out of it. He shares a little history and lore about the food we are about to eat and always throws in a couple of recipes. David's wife, Melinda, is a chef, so these combinations are consistently delicious, and I'm thrilled to be able to share a couple of them here.

My influences in the kitchen range from the East Coast church basement potlucks of my childhood to my young adulthood spent in Eastern Europe. My husband threw in his own dose of California cuisine, tempered with a touch of New York deli and the Polish shtetl. Now that we live in Minnesota, we are surrounded by delicious Southeast Asian foods, with a dash of old Scandinavia thrown in.

All of those cuisines have found their way into this book, and all of them somehow come out of a big yellow CSA box that is delivered to me every Thursday from Arkansaw, Wisconsin. They can just as easily come out of your CSA box, or your local farmers' market, or your grocery store. Whether you have a CSA share that fills you with dread, are a farmers' market junkie, pursue a quest to eat locally, or just want to eat more vegetables, I hope you'll find some inspiration here.

Chapter One

THE BASICS

ESSENTIAL KITCHEN TOOLS

A season's worth of vegetables will put your kitchen tools through a workout. You want to have your tools clean, sharp, and close at hand before you start any cooking project.

➤ Workhorses

While I'm guilty of keeping more tools in my drawers and cabinets than I really need, there are a few things that I reach for every single day. First and foremost among these is a well-sharpened **chef's knife.** Mine isn't fancy or expensive, but it is a fairly heavy-duty stainless steel number, and I get it sharpened regularly. Sharper is safer and far more pleasant to work with. (I actually have two chef's knives, because I can't imagine going a few days without my knife!) I also keep a **small serrated knife** handy whenever I'm prepping vegetables. I prefer it to a **paring knife,** but that will do as well. With those two and a **bread knife,** your cutting arsenal is complete. What you do need to have on hand are plenty of **cutting boards.** I have four plastic ones that can go in the dishwasher. I always reserve one cutting board solely for meat while I'm prepping.

If I had my druthers, every copy of this book would come with a **microplane grater.** Mine is in near-constant use (and is still sharp after half a dozen years!). It takes the zest right off citrus fruits, efficiently turns garlic and ginger into pulp, grates fresh nutmeg in a snap, and makes powder-fine grated Parmesan, which melts instantly into pesto and other dishes. Best seven dollars I've ever spent in the kitchen.

My **kitchen tongs** are also so busy that I need a backup pair. I use them to lift and turn greens while they wilt in the pan, to keep stir-fries cooking evenly, to flip vegetables as they roast in the oven—I think I get more use out of them even than a classic **wooden spoon** (though I'm always glad to have one of those handy). The other important workhorse is a **curved silicone spatula.** When I'm stirring and deglazing, its tip scrapes the bottom of the pan more efficiently than anything else. And it doesn't scratch my cast-iron pans.

Speaking of pans, none of the recipes in this book were created for nonstick pans. Teflon coating gives off dangerous fumes when heated, and the darn things always peel, anyway. I use **hard-anodized pans** (specifically a twelve-inch sauté pan with curving sides) and **cast-iron pans** (an eight-inch skillet is almost always on the stove). Food, when cooked correctly, shouldn't stick to these surfaces. Add a very light film of oil before heating the pan, and then don't be afraid to get it hot enough. A too-cool pan almost guarantees your food will stick. When your pan is hot enough to sear meats or vegetables (or perfectly fry an egg), you will see shimmers rising above the oil. Don't crowd the pan, and don't move the food until it has finished browning. If you try to lift the food and it sticks a little, give it a few more seconds and try again. Finally: no harsh metal scrubbers on your pans (I use an inexpensive **bamboo scraper**) and absolutely no soap and no soaking for your cast iron.

While it certainly is possible to wrap your freshly washed lettuce in a kitchen towel and go outside to spin it around like your grandmother did, I'm glad I don't have to dry my greens this way. I bought the biggest, toughest **salad spinner** I could find, and I'm happy to make room in my cupboards for its ample girth. And, while you might not think of it as a kitchen tool, I've got a **big, beautiful salad bowl** that makes tossing and serving salads a pleasure. To toss a salad properly, you really need a bowl about double the size of the salad itself, so your salad bowl almost can't be too big.

Two unglamorous but essential tools when it comes to cooking vegetables are a **vegetable peeler** (doesn't have to be fancy, but should be comfortable to use) and a **box grater.** Shredding changes the flavor and cooking properties of vegetables like carrots, beets, potatoes, and zucchini. I almost always prefer to grate these vegetables by hand because I don't like the long, stringy shreds the food processor makes.

➤ Nice to Have

It doesn't take much to stock a kitchen. If you've got the tools described above, along with some inexpensive **cookie sheets,** a **saucepan,** and a **Dutch oven,** you're well on your way. But there are a few things in my kitchen I'm very glad to have, even though I recognize them as indulgences.

Everything my **food processor, blender,** or **standing mixer** does my parents and grandparents once did by hand. While I like to acknowledge this to myself when I'm about to use one of these appliances, it rarely stops me from plugging them in. I also use a **stick blender** to puree soups and sauces, although it does not produce the same consistency as a standing blender.

While there are chefs out there who can cut paper-thin slices, I am not one of them. For that, I am grateful to have a **mandoline.** I also pull it out for bigger slicing and julienning jobs, but then I have to weigh the time saved slicing against the time spent washing.

A few of the recipes in this book call for deep-fat frying. There's certainly no reason to use a specialty appliance for this, but you do need a heavy-bottomed saucepan and either a **candy** or a **probe thermometer,** because the key to less greasy frying is the proper temperature.

Finally, I like to use a **kitchen scale.** While this book, like most American cookbooks, gives volumes rather than weights, it's not always very helpful to specify "two beets" or "two potatoes," for example. Beets and potatoes can be the size of golf balls or the size of softballs. When it makes a difference in the recipe, I give the weight and the volume of the prepped ingredient (two cups grated potato, for example).

➤ Secret Weapons in Your Pantry

Running short on time for dinner one night, I chopped up a cabbage, tossed it with olive oil, vinegar, salt, and pepper, and put it on the table. My family raved. I was baffled. Oil, vinegar, salt, and pepper—that's a pretty common treatment for vegetables in our house. But then I realized: I had cracked open the good stuff—the first-press, extra-virgin California olive oil from the boutique shop and the golden balsamic vinegar—overcoming my usual instinct to save such things for a special occasion. And that turned ordinary cabbage into something special.

While fresh vegetables on their own are already something special (that cabbage was young and tender and picked just days before), I keep a stash of secret weapons in my pantry that make them shine. These are the flavors that make people ask, "Ooo, what *is* that?"

Key among these are **good olive oil** and **good vinegar.** I buy the best I can afford (so good I want to drink them) and use them in small doses to kick up everyday meals. I use these as finishes—drizzling them on a dish just before serving—and deploy the inexpensive stuff for cooking. Buy small bottles in case they are not to your taste (and because olive oil does spoil).

Other great "finishes" are **coarse salt** and **freshly ground black pepper.** Always, always freshly ground pepper. Pre-ground pepper is harsh and tinny when it's fresh and dull and cardboardy when it's gone stale (which happens very quickly). And pepper grinders are pretty and fun! My grinder is adjustable, with a fine grind for pepper that will be incorporated into a dish and a very coarse one for a dramatic finish. I also prefer the taste of **kosher salt** over iodized table salt, except when the salt will be fully incorporated into the dish, as in baked goods and the like. (Many recipes here call for kosher salt. You can substitute table salt by decreasing the volume by half: 1 teaspoon of kosher salt approximately equals ½ teaspoon of table salt.) A jar of nice **sea salt** is also excellent to have on hand, for a sparing sprinkle on dishes just before serving.

While I admire people who buy all their spices whole and grind them themselves—and I encourage you to do so, if you have the inclination— that's not how I've usually chosen to spend my time in the kitchen. One exception is **whole nutmeg.** Next time you're in the spice aisle, buy a jar of whole nutmegs. Grate one on a microplane or one of those clever little nutmeg graters and take a sniff. I bet you will never buy powdered nutmeg again. Nutmeg, especially when freshly ground, is exactly the ineffable earthy flavor that bitter, dark greens like spinach, kale, and collards call out for. If all you're going to do is sauté your spinach in a pan (and I love it that way), grate a little nutmeg over top to change it from an obligatory vegetable into a *dish*.

I don't have a particularly fancy, exotic, or wide-ranging spice collection, but I've discovered a couple of especially vegetable-friendly spices I love. **Dried sumac** is often used in Middle Eastern cooking (and is easy to find at Middle Eastern grocery stores). It is a lovely purple and has a mildly woodsy tartness to it. Sumac is one way to fancy up my usual oil-vinegar-salt-and-pepper dressing. **Pimenton de la vera** is a smoked Spanish paprika that some would say is *the* flavor of Spanish cooking. I use it, however, in plenty of non-Spanish contexts, particularly on roasted vegetables and on stuffed peppers. Its deep, smoky-sweet flavor degrades when heated, so it is always added at the end of cooking.

Two of my favorite secret weapons too often get a bum rap. **Vermouth,** if you're not making a martini, seems a little déclassé, but it is my favorite deglazing liquid when making a braise. I prefer its woodsy, piney notes to white wine in most soups and in risotto. It's the secret to my favorite chicken broth. And, while anchovies are more often a punch line than a cooking ingredient these days, I always have a tube of **anchovy paste** in my pantry. Used very judiciously, it is a deep, meaty addition to vinaigrettes, and it's absolutely essential in my Roasted Scallions with Bagna Cauda (p. 74) and Bloody Mary Gazpacho (p. 109).

Two of my secret weapons don't sit in the pantry at all: I always keep a bowl of **fresh lemons and limes** on the counter. Nothing perks up vegetables like a little grated citrus zest or a squeeze of fresh juice. And, although I am hardly a gardener, I cultivate a few **pots of fresh herbs** on the front steps. Fresh herbs are so pricey in the grocery store (though a little more affordable at the farmers' market), and it's so easy to step outside with a pair of scissors and snip fresh **chives, basil, oregano, thyme, rosemary, parsley, dill,** or **cilantro** into a dish. Now, if only I could manage to keep those beauties growing inside during the winter.

CSA BASICS

Community-supported agriculture came to the United States from Europe in the mid-1980s. The idea didn't really take off, however, until the early 2000s, when a concern for local economies and independent businesses collided head-on with a growing awareness of where our food comes from. Boom! The word *locavore* was born. The process is simple: you pay in advance for a season's worth of vegetables from a farmer; you get a variety of vegetables for a set number of weeks. To find a CSA that works for you, consider a number of factors:

Cost. One of your first questions about a CSA share should be how much a season costs and how many weeks a season lasts. A weekly cost of twenty-five to thirty-five dollars is typical in the urban areas of the Upper Midwest.

You know about how much you spend on groceries each week, but what percentage of that is for vegetables? I can almost guarantee that the weekly cost of a CSA share will be more, for two reasons: that CSA box is going to change your eating habits so that you'll be eating a lot more vegetables, and those vegetables will very likely be of a much higher quality than what you find piled up in your grocery store.

The cost per pound of a CSA share—keeping in mind that that average cost is spread across dozens of kinds of vegetables—is comparable to what you would find in a natural foods co-op or Whole Foods, while, most of the time, the quality is almost incomparable. So if you're already getting most of your vegetables at high-end markets, a CSA is a good bet for you. If you do more of your shopping at a middle-of-the-road or discount supermarket, instead of comparing the cost of vegetables alone, it makes more sense to look at the weekly cost of a CSA as a percentage of your total grocery budget. It's entirely possible that the weekly cost will offset a similar amount of prepared foods and meats, which you'll eat less of once your refrigerator fills with vegetables. A CSA gets really expensive, of course, when the food goes to waste. If you don't think you can use a share by yourself, consider splitting with a friend or two for a season.

Variety. CSA farmers take real pride in providing a wide variety of vegetables each week. In our weekly box, we get eight to twelve different kinds of vegetables, more than forty across the season. Before you choose a CSA, investigate the variety of vegetables in a typical box and a typical season. You should get one or two meals' worth of each of the vegetables in any given box each week. A box full of nothing but beets—or one lonely little beet—does you no good, no matter how beautiful and tasty those beets may be.

Pick-up spot. Some CSA farmers will deliver directly to your door, but this is not the norm. Most have one central pick-up spot or maybe a handful, often at co-ops and private homes. Be realistic about your own schedule: you don't want to resent that weekly trip out of your way to pick up your vegetables. If you do find a CSA you're really interested in but don't see a spot convenient for you, ask. The farmer may know of other potential customers in your area and be willing to add a pick-up location.

Your farmer. "Our farmer": that's what we proudly call David Van Eeckhout of Hog's Back Farm in Arkansaw, Wisconsin. David had been running his own CSA farm for only a year or two when we first signed up, but he had many years of experience as an apprentice on another farm. When you choose a newer farm, you're taking a risk. CSAs, like all small businesses, often fail within the first few years. And a newer farmer hasn't had the chance to make all the mistakes a seasoned farmer has. Our risk paid off handsomely: David has turned out to be a smart, personable, hardworking, talented guy who takes immeasurable pride in filling his boxes with beautiful vegetables. But it does pay to ask about the farmer's experience and to talk to a few customers before you sign up.

Perks. Getting to know David through his warm and informative weekly newsletters and at annual farm gatherings has definitely been a perk. Ask about how the farmer communicates with members, about farm days and other gatherings, and about whether you might be welcome at the farm to have a look around. For some people, a CSA share is just a weekly box of high-quality vegetables, but others find it involves an educational component or helps create an emotional connection to food sources as well.

Organic or no? When we initially signed up for our share in Hog's Back Farm, it wasn't certified organic. But David was very open about why he hadn't earned the certification: it cost money and took time, and as a young farmer he needed to pour his money and his time into farming. He was also very open about his chemical-free farming practices, and I felt comfortable trusting him even without the imprimatur of an outside agency. He has since earned organic certification, which has undoubtedly helped him find new members. If organic certification is important to you, by all means look for a certified farm. You can also ask specific questions: What is the history of the farmland itself? How long has it been since it was farmed conventionally? What fertilizers and pest-control methods does the farmer use? How often? (Some farmers use mainly organic methods but may turn to chemicals as a last resort.) Ask about the names of specific chemicals so you can research them.

Risks. When you buy a CSA share, you're agreeing to share in the farmer's successes and failures. Beetles got the bean crop? Well, no beans for you. Bumper year for tomatoes? You get to share that joy. Most CSA farmers take their commitment to their customers very seriously no matter what odds they're battling, but they can't conjure up vegetables when a flood has taken a field.

4 REASONS NOT TO GET A CSA SHARE

1. You know what you like and you like what you know. Maybe your family likes only green beans, broccoli, and squash, and you're fine with that. Nothing wrong with that. A box of new veggies probably won't change your preferences, and you'll find yourself running to the store for the familiar stuff while your CSA share rots in the fridge.

2. You cook a couple times a week, not more. Except for the salad days of June, making full use of a CSA box requires prepping and cooking most (but not all!) nights of the week, and it will likely produce a few lunches, too. If you love to cook but only on the weekends, the farmers' market is a better bet.

3. You love the thrill of the hunt. I enjoy having vegetables come right to me, but I know people who prefer to explore the farmers' market and who will miss the weekly chance to take inspiration from what they see on the tables there. If you already have a farmers' market habit, you probably don't want to lose it.

4. You travel all summer long. The vegetables keep coming, even if you go out of town. When you travel, of course, it shouldn't be hard to find someone willing to pick up and make use of your CSA share. But do this too many times and your cost per vegetable goes up. And if you spend most summer weekends out of town, this routine can make it harder to plan meals during the week that use up all your veggies.

FARMERS' MARKET STRATEGIES

A Saturday morning idyll at the farmers' market can turn into kitchen chaos when you get home and realize you have a refrigerator full of lovely vegetables threatening to lose all their loveliness in the next few days and no idea what to make for dinner *now*. Here are a few tips for making sure you come home with exactly what you need.

Make a list. Many people love to head to the farmers' market unburdened by plans and preconceptions; they know that culinary inspiration will leap up to meet them from the colorful tables. I am not one of these people. I go with a list, much as I would to the grocery store. I know what's in season, what is at its peak, what is soon to disappear. I know what I plan to cook for the week. Sure, I have to be flexible when perfect pearls of new potatoes show up unexpectedly or the entire summer squash crop of the Upper Midwest appears to have been wiped out, but I've got a strong framework in mind.

Or make a list as you go. If you just can't bear to let go of the spontaneity of farmers' market shopping, make a "backward" shopping list. Jot down what you buy as you put it in your bag, and add a brief note next to each item: "Strawberries, jam, Sunday," "Eggplant, fries, Monday dinner." You'll know at a glance when your cooking dance card is full and it's time to just walk on by the next bit of tempting vegetal inspiration.

Know your market. Some markets require sellers to farm within a certain distance and to actually stand behind the table themselves. Some allow resellers who get their produce from the very same wholesalers the grocery stores use (you shall know them by their pineapples and avocados and by their branded cardboard boxes). If local and/or organic aren't high priorities for you, those resellers are often cheaper than grocery stores.

Walk every aisle before you buy anything. It's tempting to step up to the first table you see and start filling your bag. But buyer's remorse is right around the corner, where you might see even redder tomatoes or more tender green beans. There won't be large variations in price; farmers' market sellers know what the going rate is and tend to stick very close to it. You will, however, see variations in quantity and quality. Everybody may have their pint boxes of tomatoes marked three dollars, but if you pay attention, you'll notice that some of those boxes hold a lot more tomatoes.

Know your prices. This is tough. At the grocery store, you pay by the pound. Most often at farmers' markets—in my area, at least—you pay by the vaguely defined pint or two-pint box. If you're new to farmers' market shopping, it's a good idea to start paying attention to what, for example, a pound of green beans at your grocery store looks like. In general, for peak-season produce you'll probably find the farmers' market less expensive than your grocery store, while produce at the beginning and end of its local growing season will probably be more expensive. Freshness and quality are likely your primary reasons for shopping at the farmers' market in the first place, but we all have grocery budgets and it's advisable to know how that bag of vegetables fits yours.

Ask questions. In fact, ask stupid questions. My favorites: "What's that?" "How do you like to cook that?" "What's really good right now?" "What do you plan to bring next week?" You shouldn't feel shy about asking the people behind the table about their product. In fact, you're at the market at least in part to get closer to your food source, so "Where do you farm?" and "Do you farm organically?" are more than fair questions. Most farmers, I've found, are loquacious and passionate and happy to chat—as long as there isn't a long line behind you.

Bring cash, but a limited amount. Even—perhaps, especially—with the great prices at a farmers' market, it's easy to leave with an empty wallet and an overfilled shopping bag. Bring exactly as much as you plan to spend, and completely forget about the ATM on the premises.

Bring bags. A cart is good, too. Sellers will thank you when they can spare that added cost, and your hands will thank you when you don't have a dozen plastic bags cutting into your fingers.

Go hungry! Some of the best weekend breakfasts I've ever had have been eaten at a farmers' market. Markets and sellers have realized that shoppers come as much for the experience as for the produce, and there's nearly always at least one sausage stand or bakery.

SEASONAL SHOPPING AT YOUR GROCERY STORE

Time, as we understand it, has ceased to exist in most American grocery stores. A modern Rip Van Winkle waking up in the produce section would be hard put to guess whether there should be snow on the ground or daisies blooming outside. He would also have no idea what region of the country he was in. While this reality has saved our population from regular seasonal vitamin deficiency and catered to the whims of our taste buds in most any week, it has erased the comforting rhythms of the year.

But even die-hard farmers' market fans and off-season CSA members find themselves in the produce aisles of their local big-box grocery store every once in a while. And for many people, those chain grocery stores are what fit their budgets and schedules.

Look for "local" signs. Many stores now label produce by origin, sometimes slapping big, bright "local" stickers on items. Reward them for this practice by buying these things. If those green beans came from a local farm, they are, by definition, in season. You also get to decide what *local* means to you. Do you choose the lettuce from California over the avocado from Chile? Do you prefer to shop exclusively from farms within your state or your region? It's all about personal choices.

Watch prices. This tip is about supply and demand: abundance leads to lower prices, and peak-season vegetables are, generally speaking, abundant. Scan the store for the lowest prices per pound and take a peek; these will often be your local, in-season items.

Know your winter vegetables. There is vitamin-packed goodness to be found in storage vegetables like winter squash, sweet potatoes, onions, potatoes, and—such a blessing in the dark of winter!—hydroponic greens.

Shop the freezer aisle. Frozen vegetables—I know: crazy. Well, not so crazy. Produce is now flash frozen immediately after being picked and retains nearly all of its nutrition and flavor. Local and organic frozen foods have become very cost competitive, and the quality is generally high.

Know your priorities. Eating local, pesticide-free vegetables is very important to my family. But I've got growing kids: I can't, in good conscience, set a table devoid of anything green for six months at a time. Every year the time comes when we have used up the last of the storage vegetables from our CSA share and the last of my home-canned tomatoes and pickles, and I find myself picking up California broccoli and green beans in the grocery store. It's all about priorities.

✒ The Dirty Dozen and the Clean 15

Grocery shopping involves trade-offs. Sometimes we splurge on a beautiful fish and eat a few pasta meals that week to make up for it. Choosing vegetables is similar. If you can't buy all your groceries organic, you can put your organic dollars where they matter. The Environmental Working Group ranks fruits and vegetables by the amount of pesticides used in production and publishes two lists each year, the Dirty Dozen and the Clean 15. They recommend seeking out organic produce from the first list when possible and advise that you can feel safer buying conventional produce from the second list. This version is from 2011. See www.ewg.org for updates.

Dirty Dozen

- Apples
- Celery
- Strawberries
- Peaches
- Spinach
- Nectarines (imported)
- Grapes (imported)
- Sweet bell peppers
- Potatoes
- Blueberries (domestic)
- Lettuce
- Kale/collard greens

Clean 15

- Onions
- Corn
- Pineapples
- Avocado
- Asparagus
- Sweet peas
- Mangoes
- Eggplant
- Cantaloupe (domestic)
- Kiwi
- Cabbage
- Watermelon
- Sweet potatoes
- Grapefruit
- Mushrooms

PLANNING MEALS AROUND SEASONAL VEGETABLES

Trying to eat more vegetables, or eat in season—like most worthwhile endeavors—takes a little planning and a little prep work.

Make a menu. This is one of my personal obsessions. Every Saturday morning for the past eight years, on a little whiteboard stuck to the fridge, I have jotted down what I plan to make for dinner for the next seven dinners. We eat better, we waste less food, and we're all just a little saner for it. Because we pick up our CSA share on Thursday afternoon and our farmer always includes a list of what's (probably) coming in the next box, I know exactly what vegetables to include on my menu.

If this practice doesn't fit your lifestyle or personality, write an *à la carte* menu: a list of dishes you could make in the upcoming week. When it comes time to plan dinner, you know you have ingredients on hand for, let's say, panzanella or fennel pasta, and you get to decide which.

Shop from your fridge and freezer. Before you make a list of what you need, make a list—maybe in your head, maybe on paper—of what you've got. Use that stuff first. Some weeks you may even find you don't need to go to the grocery store at all.

Start with the vegetables. Vegetables are often an afterthought, a side dish, an obligation, something to go alongside the steak or chicken. To eat more vegetables, start with the vegetables. Begin with what's in season and what you might be craving. Maybe it's corn season and you, like me, daydream about your grandmother's corn pudding. Grandma served corn pudding alongside a Sunday roast, but you can make it the star of the show—it's got protein from egg and cheese, after all. Then braise some fennel or make a refreshing watermelon and snap pea salad.

Push meat to the side. Have some quick, easy proteins in your repertoire to round out a veggie-based meal. I, personally, think a fried egg goes with anything. Pound a chicken breast flat—less than a quarter inch thick—and cook on a hot skillet a minute or two on each side. Or make Onion-Lemon Marinated Chicken Skewers (p. 111). Throw a small skirt steak on the grill and slice it thinly. Boil white beans with herbs, garlic, and onions.

Stop thinking about mains. When I set dinner on the table, it's often hard to tell what the main dish is or what is supposed to be accompanying what. It can take some getting used to, but breaking out of the main-and-sides frame almost guarantees more variety—and more vegetables—in your diet.

Prep ahead of time. Most vegetables, especially in the late summer and fall, take a fair amount of prep work. When dinnertime has crept up on you, it's easy to glance at the cutting board and knife, sigh, and put on another pot of pasta to boil. While some vegetables, like eggplant and fennel, will go brown almost immediately when cut, others, like onions, carrots, green beans, and kale, can be chopped or sliced up to a day in advance. You'll lose a little flavor in your garlic and onions, but the time saved can be worth it. Many dishes, soups especially, can even be made start to finish the night before.

Don't forget breakfast and lunch. Most of us probably don't see a vegetable on our plates until after 6 PM. But if you're trying to make the most of a weekly CSA box or a bountiful farmers' market haul or just trying to eat more vegetables, you can't forget the other two meals of the day. Frittatas (p. 75) and hash (p. 183) are delicious, hearty weekend breakfasts. A pot of soup can make a week full of lunches. And most of the recipes in this book reheat well—or taste great at room temperature. A very common lunch in my house is last night's veggies, reheated in a skillet with a fried egg on top.

Tips for families. Nobody likes every vegetable. There are even a handful that I really don't enjoy (spaghetti squash, I'm looking at you). Often there's going to be something on the table that somebody doesn't like. The rule in my house, generally, is "tough, kiddo." But I also make sure to serve something that each person does really enjoy. Thus, I can turn a blind eye to the Vegetable Kugel (p. 80) languishing on the kids' plates because I know they're eating their green beans. On nights when I plan a particularly challenging meal—I still haven't turned the kids or even my husband on to Šaltibarščiai (p. 108)—I casually place a bowl of fruit in the center of the table and nod toward it meaningfully when I see protest starting to form on their lips.

Older kids, say seven and up, can and really should be involved in the menu planning. Make the kitchen as much their home and their province as it is yours. One night a week in our house is Kids Cook Night. They plan the meal by browsing through my cookbooks, make a shopping list, and—with a lot of supervision—cook. The only rule is there has to be at least one vegetable and some kind of protein on the table.

Tips for single people. Most of the recipes in this book generously feed a family of four, but nearly all of them can be cut in half to make one meal and one box of leftovers for a single diner. I know from experience, however, that it's not always gratifying to labor over a multi-dish dinner with no additional audience to enjoy it. When I cook for myself, I use a repertoire of basic techniques that let the vegetables shine and are easily scaled to fit my own appetite—as in Grilled Zucchini Salad (p. 69) or Pan-Fried Green Beans (p. 63). A bonus when I'm cooking for one: nobody asks, "What's the main dish?" I can pile vegetables next to vegetables and take no flak for it.

UNPACKING YOUR VEGETABLES

When you haul your vegetables into the house after a morning at the market or on CSA pick-up day, it's really tempting to just shove everything in the fridge and worry about it later. But washing and storing things properly now will keep them fresher longer and encourage you to use them faster. (A salad sounds a lot more tempting when the lettuce is clean and all you have to do is grab a few leaves and tear them up, doesn't it?)

- Rinse greens (see p. 21)
- Put potatoes and onions in a cool, dark place (like a paper bag)
- Keep garlic and hot peppers in a small bamboo steamer
- Set aside trimmings like stems and the green parts of leeks for stock
- Trim off greens from radishes, hakurei turnips, carrots, and beets, but don't discard. Beet greens are delicious cooked (see p. 136), and radish, carrot, and turnip tops are great in salads.

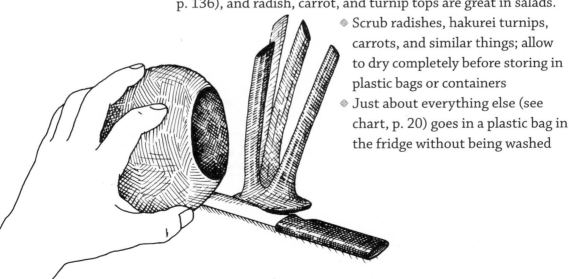

- Scrub radishes, hakurei turnips, carrots, and similar things; allow to dry completely before storing in plastic bags or containers
- Just about everything else (see chart, p. 20) goes in a plastic bag in the fridge without being washed

	BAG?	REFRIGERATOR?	WASH BEFORE STORING?	HOW LONG WILL IT KEEP?	SPECIAL INSTRUCTIONS
Arugula	Plastic	Yes	Yes	1 week	
Asparagus	Plastic	Yes	No	1–2 weeks	
Basil	Plastic	No	No	3–4 days	Will brown if refrigerated
Beets	Plastic	Yes	No	1 month	Remove tops before storing
Bitter melon	Plastic	Yes	No	1 week	
Bok choi	Plastic	Yes	No	1 week	
Broccoli	Plastic	Yes	No	1 week	
Brussels sprouts	Plastic	Yes	No	1 week	Best if eaten immediately
Cabbage	Plastic	Yes	No	2–3 weeks	
Carrots	Plastic	Yes	No	2–3 weeks	
Cauliflower	Plastic	Yes	No	1 week	
Celeriac	Plastic	Yes	No	1–2 months	
Chard	Plastic	Yes	No	1 week	Use two bags to wrap long leaves
Cilantro	No	No	No	1 week	Stand in water like cut flowers
Collard greens	Plastic	Yes	No	1 week	Use two bags for long leaves
Corn	Plastic	Yes	No	1 week	Eat immediately for best flavor
Cornmeal	Paper, wrapped in plastic	Yes	No	1 month	The fat in freshly ground whole-kernel cornmeal will go rancid
Cucumbers	Plastic	Yes	No	1 week	
Dandelion greens	Plastic	Yes	Yes	1 week	
Dill	No	No	No	1 week	Stand in water like cut flowers
Dried beans	Paper	No	No	6 months	Older beans get tough
Eggplant	Plastic	Yes	No	1 week	
Fennel	Plastic	Yes	No	1 week	
Fiddlehead ferns	Plastic	Yes	No	2–3 days	
Garlic	Paper	No	No	3–4 months	Best stored in a bamboo steamer or paper bag
Garlic scapes	Plastic	Yes	No	1 week	
Green beans	Plastic	Yes	No	1 week	
Hakurei turnips	Plastic	Yes	No	1–2 weeks	Remove tops before storing; wash tops and store separately
Kale	Plastic	Yes	No	1 week	Use two bags for long leaves
Kohlrabi	Plastic	Yes	No	1–2 weeks	Remove tops before storing
Leeks	Plastic	Yes	No	1–2 weeks	
Lettuce	Plastic	Yes	Yes	4–5 days	Use plastic bag or box; best wrap is a kitchen towel

	BAG?	REFRIGERATOR?	WASH BEFORE STORING?	HOW LONG WILL IT KEEP?	SPECIAL INSTRUCTIONS
Melon*	No	Yes	No	4–5 days	
Morels	Plastic	Yes	No	3–5 days	
Mustard greens	Plastic	Yes	Yes	1 week	
Onions	Paper	No	No	3 months	Onions will keep on the counter for a week or two, but will eventually sprout if kept in the light
Parsley	No	No	No	1 week	Stand in water like cut flowers
Parsnips	Plastic	Yes	No	1 month	
Peas	Plastic	Yes	No	1 week	
Pea shoots	Plastic	Yes	Yes	1 week	Wrap in a towel
Peppers	Plastic	Yes	No	1–2 weeks	
Potatoes	Paper	No	No	3 months	Need to be cool, dry, and in the dark or they will sprout or rot
Radishes	Plastic	Yes	No	1–2 weeks	Remove tops before storing
Ramps	Plastic	Yes	No	1 week	
Raspberries	No	Yes	No	2–3 days	Store in an open bowl in fridge; eat as soon as possible
Rhubarb	Plastic	Yes	No	1–2 weeks	
Rutabagas	Plastic	Yes	No	1–2 months	Remove tops before storing
Scallions	Plastic	Yes	Yes	1–2 weeks	Wrap in a towel
Shallots	Paper	No	No	3 months	A bamboo steamer is a good place to store
Shell beans	No	Yes	No	1–2 days	Store in an open bowl in fridge; eat as soon as possible
Spinach	Plastic	Yes	Yes	1 week	Remove stems as you wash them
Strawberries	No	Yes	No	2–3 days	Store in an open bowl in fridge; eat as soon as possible
Summer squash	Plastic	Yes	No	1–2 weeks	
Sweet potatoes	Paper	No	No	3 months	
Tomatoes	No	No	No	1 week	Store stem side down to prevent bruising
Turnips	Plastic	Yes	No	1–2 months	Remove tops before storing
Watermelon*	No	Yes	No	1 week	
Winter squash	No	No	No	1–2 months	Delicatas don't keep as long as other varieties, say 2–4 weeks
Zucchini	Plastic	Yes	No	1–2 weeks	

*Grocery store melons might keep on the counter for a couple of days; CSA melons are picked when fully ripe and need to be refrigerated immediately

Storing Garlic

The best place to store garlic is in a small bamboo steamer. It's dark, dry, and well ventilated and will keep garlic fresh for months. If your garlic does start to sprout, plant it! It will continue to grow, and you can use the green shoots, which have a mild garlic flavor. I also keep hot peppers in the same steamer, where they dry naturally without molding.

WASHING GREENS

I wash my greens in a very large bowl of cold water. (I used to do this directly in the sink, until I watched a couple of tablespoons of dirt go down the drain and thought of the cumulative effects on my pipes.) I rub each stem gently, give the whole bowl a really good swish, and then leave it alone for a few minutes so the dirt can settle. It's important to work in small batches so the dirt settles on the bottom of the bowl and not on your lettuce. Pinch off and discard tough spinach stems.

I never thought I'd love a piece of kitchen equipment as much as I do my salad spinner. I know our forefathers and foremothers dried their

greens by spinning them in kitchen towels, but they would have loved to have had a salad spinner so they didn't have to. Again, work in small batches and spin well. As you work, spread greens on clean kitchen towels so they can continue to dry.

To store, invest in several large, flat, plastic containers. Spread a kitchen towel or paper towel inside and gently layer the leaves. Moisture is both your greens' enemy and their best friend. You need to store greens in airtight containers so that they retain their own moisture, but you have to be sure that no excess moisture gets in there with them. Greens will keep about a week when stored this way, but they're really at their peak the day you bring them home. It sounds like a lot of work to keep a few boxes of greens around, but it really isn't once you figure out your rhythm. Plus you won't have to wonder what techniques are keeping the pre-bagged salad greens in the supermarket fresh.

CLEANING OUT THE CRISPER

At the height of the growing season, you're inevitably going to find a kind of traffic jam forming in your fridge. If CSA pick-up day is looming or you can't wait to get to the farmers' market and stock up on the latest in-season treats, you need to make room in the crisper drawers. And you need to do it before the quality of your vegetables starts heading seriously south. (It should go without saying that there's no point in preserving vegetables that are way past their prime or are even truly rotten. Compost those and move on.)

⊶ Pickle It

If you're adventurous, you can pickle just about anything. A quick pickle (see p. 131 for a nearly universal recipe) will preserve vegetables in the refrigerator for a few weeks, but if you want shelf-stable pickles that keep for up to a year, you'll need to pick up a good guide to home canning like the *Ball Blue Book*. Home canners should take food safety pretty seriously.

Great candidates for pickling:
- Cucumbers
- Yellow squash
- Zucchini
- Carrots

- Broccoli
- Cauliflower
- Green beans
- Mustard greens
- Chard stems
- Fennel
- Leeks

✈ Freeze It

Most vegetables need to be blanched before freezing. First, prepare the vegetables as you would want to eat them (remove tops and tails from green beans, peel and slice carrots, remove stems from greens, etc.). Boil them for one minute and then stop the cooking by plunging them into ice water or running very cold tap water over them. Shake or squeeze out as much liquid as you can and then pack into zippered plastic bags, getting as much of the air out as possible. Veggies will keep for about a month this way before getting freezer burnt, longer if you have a vacuum sealer.

Frozen vegetables do lose most of their crispness and are best suited to soups and stews after you thaw them. But that's what you want in the fall and winter, anyway.

Blanch and freeze these:
- Any dark leafy green
- Green beans
- Carrots
- Cauliflower
- Broccoli
- Sweet corn (kernels only)

Berries and fruits don't need to be blanched. Rinse and thoroughly dry them, remove pits from stone fruit, and then spread on a plate or tray in a single layer to freeze. When they're completely frozen, you can pack them into sealable plastic bags. Once again, they'll keep for just about a month unless you have a vacuum sealer.

Herbs freeze nicely in ice cube trays, minced and mixed about half and half with water. If the leaves have floated to the top while freezing, pour a thin layer of water over the top and freeze again, to protect them from freezer burn.

To freeze winter squash, bake it (see method on p. 138) and spoon the flesh into plastic bags or plastic containers, being sure to remove as much air as possible.

My grandmother taught me the trick to freezing tomatoes. Just put them in the freezer. Just like that, whole. In a plastic bag if you feel like it. When you're ready to use one, hold it under warm water until the skin comes off easily, then let it sit on the counter to thaw completely. Remove the core with a sharp knife, and then use it in any recipe that calls for canned tomatoes.

➤ Can It

Canning is a fun and (often) economical way to preserve vegetables, but it's not one that anyone should undertake without expert written guidance. Seek out reputable canning books from Ball (the manufacturer of Mason jars) or a university extension service. Keep in mind that high-acid foods like pickles, tomatoes, and some fruits can be preserved in a boiling water canner, but for low-acid foods you'll need a pressure canner.

➤ Bake It

Preserving vegetables is a great excuse to whip up some desserts. And fresh baked goods are a lot easier to give away to friends and neighbors than baskets of zucchini.

Zucchini Bread (p. 86) and Pumpkin Bread (p. 185) freeze very well when double-wrapped in aluminum foil. (Just put them in the fridge overnight to thaw.) Parsnip Cake (p. 186) and Spiced Chocolate Beet Cake (p. 152) also freeze well when left in their baking pans. Let cool completely, then coat a sheet of plastic wrap with nonstick spray and place it directly on the surface of the cake before wrapping the whole thing in two layers of aluminum foil. Pumpkin Bread Pancakes (p. 184) are also a great way to use up veggies.

➤ Dry It

Dry herbs by tying them into loose bundles and hanging in a breezy place for a week or so. You can also spread them in a single layer on a baking sheet and put it out of the way for several days. Store in airtight containers.

To dry hot peppers, slice in half lengthwise, spread in a single layer on a baking sheet, and place them in a 200-degree oven for a couple of hours. The time will depend on the size and moisture content of your peppers. Take them out when they are crispy but before they brown. Store in a glass jar.

It is absolutely essential to be sure that herbs and peppers are completely moisture free before sealing them in airtight containers. Otherwise, a nasty mold will develop.

➤ Make Stock

Stock is an excellent option for vegetables on the verge of going bad—definitely not rotten, but no longer crisp and appealing. Simmer—don't boil—in plenty of water, covered, for about an hour.

➤ Make Pesto

If it's green and leafy, you can turn it into pesto. See p. 91 for a master recipe and more pesto uses. If you're going to freeze your pesto—and I highly recommend that you stock your freezer with plenty of pesto—leave out the cheese and add it after you thaw it.

Excellent pesto ingredients:
- Spinach
- Arugula
- Parsley
- Garlic scapes
- Ramps
- Shiso
- Fennel
- Pea shoots

Chapter Two

SPRING (APRIL TO MAY)

In our seasonless world, where nearly every fruit and vegetable can be flown in from somewhere, there are few truly seasonal foods left. Most of those—ones you can't get for love or money at the wrong time of year, no matter how much you compromise on quality—arrive in the early spring. Without my annual spring taste of **ramps, pea shoots, morel mushrooms, fiddleheads,** and **garlic scapes,** I feel a little bit like I cheated myself. The dish doesn't have to be fancy, but make plans to enjoy each of these before it disappears.

As thrilled as I am to see the first **asparagus** and **rhubarb** arrive, I always feel sated before their seasons end. Fortunately, they're both very easy to cook and to work into just about any meal, so we eat a lot of **Roasted Asparagus with Chive-Egg Sauce** (p. 41) and savor sodas made with **Rhubarb Syrup** (p. 55).

Fresh green things are rare and precious sights at the market in early spring. Market vegetables are still side dishes, and my family eats a lot more meat-based meals, as we tend to do in the winter. This is also a good time to seek out dried beans like **favas. Braised Bok Choi** (p. 39) or **Sautéed Hakurei Turnips** (p. 38) alongside a dish of seasoned farro, brown rice, or lentils is also a common dinner. **Ramp** or **Garlic Scape Pesto** (p. 34) tossed with pasta or spread on a sandwich makes a terrific lunch.

Late spring truly marks the beginning of our salad days. The first several CSA boxes of the year include three, four, or even five heads of lettuce. Farmers' market lettuces will also call out from the stalls, and I inevitably pop into the bag one or two more than I had really planned for. That means salads every night of the week, so I keep feta and blue cheese, boiled eggs, hard sausage, salted nuts, and good oil and vinegar on hand—along with **homemade croutons** and **salad dressing**—so that mealtime never becomes a chore.

Spring MENUS

Combinations that highlight the season's best

What's in Season

Arugula	Hakurei turnips	Pea shoots
Asparagus	Herbs	Radishes
Bok choi	Honey	Ramps
Dandelion greens	Lettuce	Rhubarb
Fiddlehead ferns	Morels	Spinach
Garlic scapes	Mustard greens	

HOW TO DRESS A SALAD

I don't believe in dressing "on the side." This practice yields gloppy, uneven dressing and always puts me in mind of sad banquet salads with passed boats of syrupy raspberry vinaigrette. Dressing your salad before serving allows you to coat the greens perfectly.

I'm a purist: I like nothing better than just greens and dressing in my salads. But if you wish to add extras like cucumbers and onions, be sure everything is bite size.

1. Tear lettuce into bite-size pieces, about one inch. Big pieces, or even whole lettuce leaves, are pretty to look at but not very pretty to watch someone eat. Snip some fresh herbs—chives, tarragon, basil—in with the lettuce.

2. Wait to dress your salad until just before serving. I believe it was Mark Bittman who said that every diner should be in his or her chair, with forks raised, before the dressing touches the leaves. I do have an exception to this rule: I dress tougher greens, like radish and turnip tops, about five minutes before serving, because it takes a little longer for the flavor to penetrate.

3. Use a very big bowl, at least twice as big as the volume of lettuce.

4. I find that a scant tablespoon per cup of greens is the right ratio. Don't overdress! Place the dressing in the bottom of the bowl and the lettuce on top.

5. Using two large implements, very gently scoop from the bottom and lightly toss the lettuce upward. Do this a few more times than you think is necessary, to be sure every surface is thoroughly coated.

There are several dressing recipes on p. 30–32, but all you need for a delicious salad is good olive oil—and by "good" I mean so good you want to drink it—vinegar or lemon juice, salt, and pepper. First toss the lettuce thoroughly with the oil and then toss again with the vinegar, and finally with the salt and pepper.

My favorite way to dress a salad, however, is with a freshly poached egg, cooked so that the yolk is still very runny. Top two to three cups of torn greens with the egg, a tiny drizzle of olive oil, and a pinch of salt and pepper. Toss very well with two forks, breaking up the egg and allowing it to coat the greens.

CONDIMENTS AND SALAD TOPPINGS

Never-Buy-Croutons-Again Croutons

Croutons are one of those things I think many people have looked at on the grocery shelf and thought, "Why don't I make those? They're just toasted bread." Yes, yes they are. Still, I used to toss them into the cart anyway, because it seemed like such a hassle.

For this spring's salad season, though, I'm willing to bet you'll finally give up your store-bought crouton habit. I stumbled on this solution by accident: I threw a grilling party and went a bit over the top in my supplies. Hence, my secret crouton source: hamburger and hot dog buns. They are exactly the right texture to soak up the oil and crisp up consistently in the oven, with no pesky tough crusts. I stash extras in the freezer and pull them out (they'll thaw in about half an hour) when I want to make a salad.

Don't substitute fresh herbs as is; they'll burn in the oven. If fresh herbs are all you have on hand, spread them on a parchment-lined baking sheet and dry them in the oven as it is preheating, about ten minutes. Crush before adding.

6 hamburger or hot dog buns

¼ cup olive oil

½ teaspoon kosher salt

¼ teaspoon freshly ground black pepper

1 teaspoon dried oregano

1 teaspoon dried basil

1 teaspoon dried thyme

Heat oven to 375 degrees. Separate tops and bottoms of buns. Slice each hot dog bun piece in half lengthwise and then in quarters crosswise (to make 16 croutons from each bun) and each hamburger bun piece into 9 more or less even cubes. This makes jumbo croutons, which is the way I like them. You can cut them smaller, of course.

Combine olive oil, salt, pepper, and herbs in a very large mixing bowl. Using a spatula, spread the oil mixture up the sides of the bowl and add the sliced buns. Stir very quickly, scraping sides and bottom of bowl. The buns will soak up the oil the second they touch it, and you want them to be coated as evenly as possible.

Spread croutons in a single layer on a rimmed baking sheet. Bake, stirring occasionally, until golden brown and crispy on all sides, about 20 minutes. Store in an airtight container up to 3 days. Makes about 6 cups.

Goat Cheese Dressing

Aggressive greens like turnip and radish tops need a bold dressing like this one. It's tangy, tart, and creamy, and every drop is packed with flavor, so you really don't want to go overboard. Toasted walnuts are a great addition.

2 ounces goat cheese

3 tablespoons mayonnaise (p. 133)

¼ cup lemon juice

1 generous tablespoon finely minced fresh thyme

1 generous tablespoon finely minced fresh oregano

pinch salt

freshly ground black pepper

Mix the goat cheese and mayonnaise in a small bowl, mashing with a fork to blend it all really well. Whisk in remaining ingredients.

Makes about ¾ cup, enough for 2 large bowls of greens. This dressing is best used right away but will keep in the refrigerator for a day or two. It will separate, so you'll need to whisk it back together.

Honey-Lemon Vinaigrette

The proportions in this recipe are simple (and therefore easy for me to remember as I rush to get dinner on the table), but I think they're like the golden mean: mathematically meant to be. This dressing is sweet and tart and warmly spicy with the garlic, so it might overwhelm more delicate greens like butter leaf or Bibb lettuces. It really stands up well to heartier and more bitter greens, like radish and turnip tops, and even dresses up workaday lettuces like romaine.

2 tablespoons honey

2 tablespoons freshly squeezed lemon juice

2 tablespoons olive oil

1 clove garlic, grated on a microplane or pressed through a garlic press

¼ teaspoon salt

plenty of freshly ground black pepper

Combine all ingredients in a small jar. Shake well and toss with hearty greens like radish or turnip tops. Makes ⅜ cup.

Basic Creamy Dressing

Mild and homey, just a little sweet and a little tart, this dressing is great on more delicate greens, like Bibb and green leaf lettuce. Chives and fresh oregano are nice substitutions for the basil. Also, my family likes a lot of pepper, so you may want to adjust for your taste.

> 2 tablespoons mayonnaise (p. 133)
>
> 3 tablespoons buttermilk
>
> ⅛ teaspoon sugar
>
> 2 tablespoons minced fresh basil
>
> 1 teaspoon lemon juice
>
> 1 teaspoon freshly ground black pepper

Mix mayonnaise and buttermilk in a small bowl, mashing with a fork to fully incorporate. Add remaining ingredients and mix well. Let sit about half an hour or so for the flavors to develop. Makes ½ cup.

Peppercorn Parmesan Dressing

This bold dressing is perfect for strong, bitter greens like dandelion greens, turnip tops, and escarole or a mixture of arugula and romaine. I like pink peppercorns for their floral flavor, but black ones make a nice dressing as well.

> 1 tablespoon pink peppercorns
>
> 3 egg yolks
>
> 3 tablespoons white vinegar
>
> ½ teaspoon kosher salt
>
> ¼ cup half-and-half
>
> ¼ cup Parmesan, grated on a microplane (1 ounce)

Pulse peppercorns quickly in a coffee grinder or grind with a mortar and pestle. (You can also put the peppercorns in a plastic bag and whack them with a rolling pin.) Whisk egg yolks, vinegar, and salt with peppercorns in a glass bowl. Over a pot of water kept just at a simmer, place glass bowl (you can also use a double boiler) and cook, whisking constantly, until thickened like cream, about 3 to 4 minutes. Remove from heat and whisk in half-and-half. Stir in Parmesan. Makes ¾ cup.

Ramp and Mushroom Pesto

Replacing the nuts in a traditional pesto with mushrooms gives it a creamier flavor with no grit. This intensely garlicky spread is tasty on crusty bread, spooned over eggs, in a grilled cheese sandwich, or spread over pizza crust.

½ cup olive oil, divided

6 ounces crimini mushrooms, brushed clean and finely chopped (about 3 cups)

½ teaspoon kosher salt

6 ounces ramps, trimmed and roughly chopped (about 4 cups)

½ cup finely grated Parmesan (2 ounces)

salt to taste

Pour 1 tablespoon of the olive oil into a large sauté pan and place over medium-high heat. Add mushrooms and kosher salt. Cook, stirring occasionally, until mushrooms brown and liquid has completely evaporated, about 8 to 10 minutes. Remove from heat and cool slightly.

Place ramps in bowl of food processor with cooked mushrooms. With blade running, slowly pour remaining oil through feed tube to yield a rough paste. Stir Parmesan into pesto; taste and adjust salt. Makes a scant 2 cups.

Garlic Scape Pesto

Garlic scapes are almost magical. They have the bite of garlic and the fresh green flavor of a delicate herb, all in one. And, like magical creatures, they disappear in the blink of an eye. This pesto is a great way not only to enjoy them now but to preserve their flavor for later. It freezes well in small portions. If you're going to freeze it, I recommend leaving out the Parmesan and stirring it in after thawing.

> **1 cup roughly chopped garlic scapes**
>
> **½ cup roughly chopped walnuts**
>
> **½ cup olive oil**
>
> **½ cup finely grated Parmesan (2 ounces)**
>
> **½ teaspoon kosher salt, or to taste**

Place garlic scapes and walnuts in bowl of food processor. With blade running, pour olive oil through feed tube. Add more olive oil if you prefer a thinner pesto rather than a spreadable one. Remove mixture to a small bowl and stir in Parmesan. Taste before adding salt, as some cheese is saltier than others. Makes about 1½ cups.

Pickled Mustard Greens

At my local markets, these beloved Hmong greens (zaub ntsuab) are labeled "mustard greens," "mustard cabbage," "bamboo cabbage," and about a half a dozen other things. Look for long, thin, dark green leaves with relatively thick stems and tiny yellowish flower buds. They're great in a stir-fry, and their slightly bitter flavor works well with all kinds of pork.

This is a fermented pickle that will keep in the refrigerator for several months (this recipe has not been tested for home canning), but if you're more comfortable with a brined pickle, use the recipe on p. 131.

4 cups water

2 tablespoons salt

1 tablespoon sugar

1 dried red pepper

1 large bunch mustard greens, rinsed, cut into 1-inch pieces
(to yield 4 cups)

Mix together first 4 ingredients (water through pepper), being sure to
dissolve sugar and salt. Stir in mustard greens. Place mixture in a scru-
pulously clean opaque bowl and cover with a plate, weighted down if
necessary. You don't want an airtight seal, but you do want to be sure
that all of the mustard greens stay submerged. (A pickling crock is, of
course, ideal, but you can approximate one with a bowl and plate.) Keep
in a cool, dark place for 3 days. Transfer to jars with tight-fitting lids and
store in the refrigerator for up to 3 months. Makes about 4 cups.

Hmong Farmers and Southeast Asian Vegetables

Garrison Keillor may joke about Norwegian bachelor farmers on *A
Prairie Home Companion,* but the face of farming in Minnesota and
Wisconsin is increasingly Southeast Asian. Hmong families began
settling in the upper Midwest in the 1970s, after the United States
withdrew from Vietnam, and have come in several waves since then.
Many have continued farming as they once did in Laos. At farmers'
markets here in the Twin Cities, more than half the stalls may be run
by Hmong family farms.

These farms produce a remarkably diverse array of vegetables—
no monoculture here!—and most of the produce on display is uni-
versally familiar. But mixed in among the broccoli, lettuce, and potatoes are less-familiar items important in Hmong cuisine. One of my
favorites, and perhaps the most easily adaptable to western dishes,
is **mustard greens.** Mustard greens are among the first green things
to appear in the spring, and they are a steady presence in the market

through the fall. **Pickled Mustard Greens** (p. 34) are a traditional accompaniment to a plate of meat and rice or with Korean-inspired **Midwestern Bibimbap** (p. 50).

Bitter melon is a common sight later in the year. Beloved for its intensely bitter flavor, it can take some getting used to for those of us who didn't grow up with it. A sweet, sour, spicy **Bitter Melon and Chicken Stir-Fry** (p. 148) reins in some of the bitterness and showcases the melon's crunchy texture.

At Hmong market stalls you'll also find big, gangly bunches of **chrysanthemum greens, eggplants** of all shapes and sizes, some no bigger than a golf ball (surprisingly tasty raw), and rows and rows of **basil,** more kinds than you ever knew existed. When something catches your eye, just ask the grower what he or she does with it.

SALADS AND OTHER SIDES

Mashed Fava Beans on Grilled Rye Bread

Favas are easy to love: they're meaty and mild and soak up flavors like olive oil and rosemary. In the very early spring, while you're waiting for fresh fava beans to make their blink-and-you'll-miss-it appearance at the market late in the summer, pureed dried favas make a nice substitute.

1 cup dried fava beans

½ teaspoon kosher salt

freshly ground black pepper

leaves from 1 sprig rosemary, plus more for garnish

1 cup olive oil, plus more for grilling

sliced rye bread

Soak fava beans in water for 6 to 12 hours, until skins come off easily (this takes longer for older beans). Use your fingers to pry off the skins and discard them. Boil beans 30 minutes, until very soft. Place in bowl of food processor with salt, pepper, and rosemary. With blade running, pour olive oil through feed tube and process until very smooth. Makes 3 cups. Freezes well.

Brush bread with olive oil and toast on hot grill or griddle pan. Cover liberally with fava spread; garnish with rosemary.

Hakurei Turnip Slaw

Hakurei turnips are nothing like their dense, starchy cousins. This Japanese variety, also known as salad turnips, *is crisp and refreshing like radishes. And, like radishes, they are easy to enjoy raw and have a little bit (sometimes a lot) of peppery bite. This easy slaw is tasty as a side dish but is also terrific as a condiment. Try some on a bratwurst, hot dog, or burger, and you may never reach for jarred relish again.*

If you buy turnips with the tops on, be sure to save the greens for a hearty salad.

1 bunch green onions (about 10 fat ones)

2 cups peeled, grated hakurei turnips

2 tablespoons rice vinegar

2 tablespoons rice wine (mirin)

1 teaspoon kosher salt

plenty of freshly ground black pepper

Slice white parts of green onions, reserving green parts for another use. Mix together all ingredients. Serve immediately or refrigerate for up to 3 days. The flavor will sharpen over time. Makes about 3 cups.

Speedy Sautéed Hakurei Turnips and Greens

SERVES 4

This recipe is a favorite from the newsletter of my CSA farmer, David Van Eeckhout. Without it, I might never have guessed that turnip greens are not only edible but quite tasty. I also might never have tried cooking the turnips, because we end up eating most of them in raw wedges or in the slaw on p. 37.

> **1 bunch hakurei turnips with greens (about 6 medium turnips)**
>
> **2 teaspoons olive oil**
>
> **1 teaspoon butter**
>
> **salt and freshly ground black pepper to taste**
>
> **2 tablespoons white wine**

Cut greens from bulbs; rinse well but do not dry aggressively. Slice greens into 2-inch pieces. Scrub bulbs well, rubbing to remove any dirt. Trim and discard roots and tough top. Cut each bulb into 8 wedges.

Heat olive oil and butter in a wide sauté pan with a lid over medium-high heat until butter has melted and bubbling has subsided. Add turnip wedges and sprinkle lightly with salt and pepper. Cook until crisp tender, about 5 minutes. Remove turnips from pan and set aside.

Add greens to pan. Cover and cook until just tender, 6 to 8 minutes. Add wine and cook, uncovered, until liquid is nearly gone. Return turnips to pan and heat through. Serve immediately.

Overwintered Vegetables

Before the growing season begins in earnest, the farmers' markets can look an awful lot like fall. Some farmers overwinter hardy crops like **parsnips, carrots, broccoli, cauliflower,** and **spinach** by planting in the fall and keeping them mulched through the coldest months. They may also have some storage crops like **potatoes, sweet potatoes, winter squash,** and **onions** left to sell. With the weather still brisk, it's a good time to try out fall recipes from Chapter Six, like **Squash Chili** (p. 177), **Sweet Potato Blue Cheese Soup** (p. 173), and **Roasted Carrots and Parsnips** (p. 168).

Braised Bok Choi

SERVES 4

Bok choi, when very fresh, is tasty raw, sliced thin, but it really sings when simmered until tender in this slightly sweet, slightly salty sauce. Both baby bok choi and the mature variety work well here. Cut larger leaves in half lengthwise and cook them a bit longer.

> 1 tablespoon sesame oil
>
> 2 cloves garlic, thinly sliced
>
> 1 pound bok choi, rinsed, leaves separated
>
> 1 tablespoon packed brown sugar
>
> 2 tablespoons soy sauce
>
> 1 cup no-sodium chicken or vegetable broth

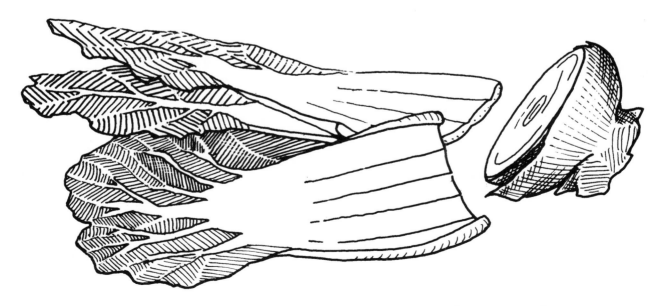

Pour sesame oil into a wide pan and add garlic. Heat over medium-high heat until shimmering. Push garlic to a cooler side of the pan and add half the bok choi leaves. Stir quickly and then let brown about 1 minute. Push to side of pan and repeat with remaining bok choi.

Dissolve sugar in soy sauce and add to pan along with broth. Bring to a light boil. Simmer, uncovered, until bok choi is tender, about 4 minutes for baby bok choi and 7 minutes for larger bok choi. Sauce will reduce slightly. Taste and add salt if necessary, although I find that the soy sauce is salty enough. Serve immediately, as bok choi will continue to give off liquid.

Baked Spinach

SERVES 4

When late spring evenings are still chilly, warm spinach is a comforting and hearty choice. What kind of cheese you use is up to you. I like something with a lot of flavor—blue cheese and feta work well—or a mix of Parmesan and fontina.

> 1 tablespoon butter
>
> 2 pounds spinach, stems removed, leaves roughly chopped
>
> 1 teaspoon kosher salt
>
> 1 egg
>
> 3 tablespoons fresh bread crumbs
>
> 2 ounces cheese, grated or crumbled (see head note)

Heat oven to 450 degrees. Melt butter in wide sauté pan over medium-high heat. Add spinach in batches, sprinkling each batch lightly with salt. Turn spinach with tongs and cook just until it wilts, a minute or less. Lift cooked spinach out of the pan into a small baking dish, squeezing to leave behind as much liquid as possible. Drain liquid from pan between batches.

Beat egg lightly with bread crumbs. Spoon mixture over spinach. Sprinkle with cheese and bake 10 to 12 minutes.

Roasted Asparagus
with Chive-Egg Sauce

SERVES 4

While steaming is the most common way to cook asparagus, I much prefer it roasted. In a hot oven, the stalks turn blistery and brown on the outside and creamy on the inside—rather than flabby all the way through. While I happily eat these right out of the pan with my fingers, if you and your family prefer to actually sit down and eat your dinner with forks, the egg sauce is the perfect accompaniment.

1 pound asparagus, trimmed and peeled (see note, p. 42)

1 teaspoon olive oil

½ teaspoon kosher salt

2 hard-cooked eggs, finely chopped (or passed twice through an egg slicer)

2 tablespoons butter, melted

2 tablespoons minced chives

salt and freshly ground black pepper to taste

freshly squeezed lemon juice

Heat oven to 500 degrees. Place asparagus in an oven-safe dish large enough to hold it in more or less a single layer. Drizzle with oil and massage it in well with your hands. Sprinkle with salt. Roast 20 minutes, until asparagus starts to blister.

Meanwhile, make the sauce. Mix eggs, melted butter, chives, salt, and pepper in a small bowl. Squeeze a little lemon juice over the asparagus as soon as you pull it out of the oven, so it sizzles in the pan. Remove to a serving dish and spoon egg sauce over top.

Asparagus Appeal

Is the best asparagus fat or thin? If this perennial debate ever comes up at your table, you can look sagely at both parties and proclaim, "You're right!" Asparagus spears don't start out thin and get fat (thus fat spears *aren't* old and tough, as you might think). Instead, each spear, depending on where it's growing in its own individual plant, is destined to be either fat or thin.

Which you buy depends on what looks best in the market (I'll take the freshest spears any day, regardless of girth) and what you plan to do with them. For a raw asparagus salad, thinner spears are more elegant, while for roasting I prefer the fattest spears I can find (more creamy goodness on the inside). What's most important is consistency. Look for bundles of asparagus with spears that are all more or less the same size.

Peeling, too, is a matter of personal preference. I tend to peel spears that are much fatter than a pencil, but sometimes I'm too lazy to do even that. Before I trim the ends, I grab one spear and snap off the woody part and use that as a guide to trim the rest of the bunch, rather than snapping each individual spear.

Dandelion Salad

SERVES 4

Dandelions can be intensely bitter, especially when cooked. (I learned that lesson the hard way once when making a stir-fry.) This cooked dressing softens them up just a little bit without drawing out the really frighteningly bitter undertones. The cooked onions add a necessary sweetness. I recommend choosing a fruity wine that's not too dry, like a California chardonnay, to play up that sweet note. Shavings of a nutty, mellow cheese keep the whole dish grounded.

> **1 (8-ounce) bunch dandelion greens, stems trimmed, leaves sliced into 1-inch pieces**
>
> **¼ cup olive oil**

½ red onion, sliced in very thin half moons

½ teaspoon kosher salt

½ cup white wine

½ cup champagne vinegar

freshly ground black pepper to taste

1 ounce Parmesan or other hard cheese, shaved paper thin

Place dandelion leaves in a large serving bowl. Combine olive oil, onions, and salt in a small sauté pan over medium-low heat and cook 10 minutes, until softened but not soggy. Add wine, increase heat to medium-high, and cook until the liquid has reduced by at least half. Add vinegar and pepper to pan. Heat through and pour immediately over greens. Toss well. Sprinkle with Parmesan and serve hot.

Big Salad

SERVES 4

In my house, Big Salad (all my attempts to rechristen it have failed) is a springtime favorite. Little do the happy salad-eaters know that this is my favorite way of cleaning out the crisper. It's all about the presentation. I get out my prettiest platter and make it look festive. I shred the lettuce to make it more attractive and to be sure a little lettuce makes it into every bite. Then I alternate the desirable toppings (the eggs, meat, and cheese) with the vegetables. Serving with kitchen tongs allows each person to take exactly what they want (along with plenty of lettuce) and toss with their own oil-and-vinegar dressing on the plate.

Favorite salad additions, depending on the season: radishes (cut into matchsticks), cooked potatoes, green beans (raw, cut into 1-inch pieces), bean sprouts, cooked beets (cut into matchsticks), shredded carrots, tomato wedges, cucumbers and zucchini (also matchsticks), kernels from leftover corn on the cob, chickpeas—I actually can think of very few veggies I haven't put on a Big Salad.

1 large head lettuce, leaves separated and rinsed

½ cup crumbled cooked bacon, cubed salami, or other salty cured meat

4 ounces cheese, cut into ¼-inch cubes

3–4 hardboiled eggs, passed through an egg slicer

¾–1 cup each of three different vegetables (see head note)

very good olive oil

nice balsamic vinegar

lemon or lime wedges

kosher salt

freshly ground black pepper

Stack lettuce leaves and fold in half. Use a sharp knife to slice into thin (less than ¼-inch wide) strips. Spread on large plate or platter. Arrange toppings (meat through vegetables) in neat wedges or stripes across the top. Serve with tongs, passing olive oil, vinegar or citrus, salt, and pepper.

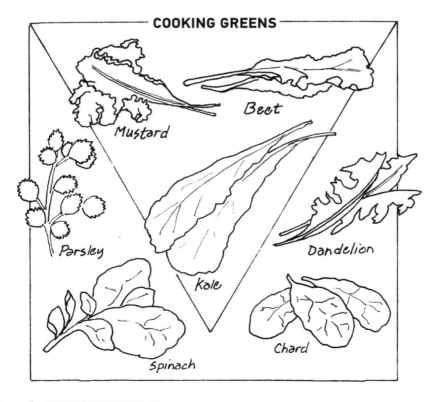

COOKING GREENS

Mustard

Beet

Parsley

Dandelion

Kale

Spinach

Chard

Spring Ramp and Mushroom Soup

SERVES 4

This is not a pretty soup; it turns out a muddy green. But its flavor is so intensely rich, earthy, and springlike that it's worth getting past its appearance. A dollop of sour cream or some finely chopped green onions as garnish will help pretty it up.

This soup relies heavily on flavorful mushrooms to complement the garlicky ramps, so avoid white button mushrooms. Criminis are a fine choice, but a mix of whatever forest mushrooms you can find in the market is best.

> 4 tablespoons (½ stick) butter, divided
>
> 1 pound mushrooms (see head note), brushed clean and finely chopped
>
> ½ teaspoon kosher salt
>
> 6 ounces ramps
>
> 4 cups water
>
> 3 tablespoons flour

Melt 2 tablespoons of the butter in a large sauté pan over medium-high heat. Toss mushrooms with salt and add to butter, spreading in a thin layer over the bottom of the pan. (Work in batches if your pan is small; crowding the mushrooms will keep them from browning.) Cook, stirring occasionally, until mushrooms are brown and liquid has evaporated, about 12 to 15 minutes.

Meanwhile, slice ramps thinly, separating white ends from green tops. Add ends to pan with mushrooms and cook until fragrant, about 1 minute. Add ramp tops and water and bring to a boil. Simmer, covered, 20 minutes.

Meanwhile, melt remaining 2 tablespoons butter in a separate small saucepan over medium heat. Cook until bubbling subsides but don't let butter brown. Stir in flour and cook, stirring constantly, to make a thick paste, about 1 minute. Whisk this roux into simmering soup and stir thoroughly until slightly thickened, about 3 to 4 minutes. Taste and adjust seasoning. Use a stick blender to puree the soup, or carefully transfer liquid to a standing blender to puree in batches. (If you use a standing blender, fill the pitcher no more than halfway and then place a dish towel over the lid and hold it down firmly with your hand. Hot liquids in a blender can explode.) Makes about 1 quart.

MOSTLY MAIN DISHES

Pea Shoot Pesto Pasta Salad

SERVES 4

Each week during CSA season, we get two treats: one is a big box of lovingly grown and picked vegetables; the other is the witty, warm, and informative newsletter that comes with it. Farmer David Van Eeckhout always includes a couple of recipes, many developed by his wife, Melinda, a chef. Some of these have become family favorites. This light, springy pesto—so much brighter than its late-summer basil cousin—is almost always the fate of the first bunch of pea shoots to arrive each year. It's also a fantastic ingredient on its own and great on toast, in vegetable soups, or atop a fried egg.

½ cup walnuts

1 bunch pea shoots (about 4 cups)

1 clove garlic

¼ cup olive oil

1 teaspoon kosher salt

½ cup freshly grated Parmesan (2 ounces)

12 ounces pasta (orecchiette and fusilli are good choices)

8 ounces cherry tomatoes, halved

Combine first 6 ingredients (walnuts through Parmesan) in bowl of food processor and process until you have a nice green paste. Pour a little more olive oil down the feed tube while it's processing if you like a thinner pesto.

Cook pasta according to package directions, in generously salted water. Combine cooked pasta with pesto. Let cool completely. Stir in cherry tomatoes and serve at room temperature.

Asparagus Soufflé

SERVES 4

If soufflé *sounds too intimidating, then call this* spoonbread, *as a cornmeal pudding might be called in the South. That's the way you should serve it, too, in big homey spoonfuls, a light, springy green, with nibbly bits of asparagus tops throughout.*

You don't have to use a soufflé dish, but choose something with a two-quart capacity (the batter should fill it no more than halfway, as it will puff up) and greatly reduce the baking time for a shallower dish.

1 pound asparagus

2 cups milk (2% works best)

1½ tablespoons unsalted butter

½ teaspoon salt

½ cup cornmeal

3 eggs, separated

1 teaspoon cream of tartar

Heat oven to 400 degrees. Coat a 2-quart soufflé dish or other deep baking dish with cooking spray or butter.

Peel the asparagus if it's much thicker than a pencil. Snap off tough bottoms and discard. Cut off tops, chop roughly, and reserve. Chop remaining stems into ¼-inch pieces.

In a heavy saucepan set over medium heat, warm milk until tiny bubbles just start to appear around the edges. Add butter, salt, and chopped asparagus stems. Very slowly sprinkle in cornmeal, whisking constantly to avoid lumps. Continue whisking and cook 5 minutes, until cornmeal is thick and nearly smooth. Puree with stick blender or transfer mixture in batches to puree in a standing blender.

Cool mixture until you can comfortably hold a finger in the cornmeal for 10 to 20 seconds. Stir in egg yolks and asparagus tops. Set aside.

Beat the egg whites with the cream of tartar until they hold stiff peaks. Stir about a cup of the egg whites into the cornmeal mixture to lighten it, then fold in the rest by gently pouring the egg whites on top of the cornmeal, inserting a wide spatula into the middle of the mixture, scooping toward you, and folding it back on itself. Gently spoon mixture into prepared pan. Place in oven and immediately reduce heat to 375 degrees. Cook 45 minutes, until brown and puffy and a skewer inserted into the middle comes out clean.

Variation: Add ½ cup grated Parmesan along with egg yolks.

Lettuce Cups

SERVES 4

When I daydream about that first CSA box of the season, which is usually stuffed with fat, fresh heads of lettuce, this is one of the meals I'm thinking about. If there's Bibb lettuce in the box, I nearly always make lettuce cups that very evening, to take advantage of its just-picked flavor and crispness. I first found this recipe on a message board for new mothers when my kids were tiny. I revised it and made it part of my repertoire and only later learned that I had been cooking Nigella Lawson's Thai Crumbled Beef in Lettuce Cups. So I offer my version here with deep gratitude to Nigella for nearly a decade of perfect spring meals.

Oh, and yes, fish sauce straight out of the bottle smells like dirty socks, but don't be tempted to skip this ingredient. Once it cooks into the meat, it deepens the flavor, and the dish lacks something without it. If you use ground turkey, don't choose extra lean, as it will turn out rubbery.

1 tablespoon vegetable oil

1 pound ground beef or turkey

2 tablespoons fish sauce

2 tablespoons freshly squeezed lime juice

2 tablespoons soy sauce

¼ cup sliced fresh basil or chopped fresh cilantro

1 small bunch green onions, white and green parts, finely sliced (about 1 cup)

1 very small serrano or other hot pepper, minced

1 large head Bibb or romaine lettuce, leaves separated and gently rinsed

Heat oil in a large sauté pan over medium heat. Add meat and cook until no longer pink. Add fish sauce and cook until all liquid is gone from the pan, then cook a minute or two longer, until mixture starts to brown.

Meanwhile, stir together next 5 ingredients (lime juice through pepper) in a large serving bowl. Add hot meat and stir well. Serve warm, with a separate bowl of whole lettuce leaves so everyone can fill their own lettuce cups.

Midwestern Bibimbap

SERVES 1

My favorite use for pickled mustard greens is in my own simplified version of bibimbap. Classic Korean comfort food, bibimbap *is "all mixed up." It comes to the table as a lovely composition of pickled vegetables and rice, and then the diner gets to do the mixing up. If you're lucky, a Korean restaurant will serve it in a hot stone bowl—*dolsot bibimbap—*that cooks the rice and egg to form a tasty crunchy crust on the bottom. Many versions include sautéed beef or chicken, but for a quick supper for one, I stick with just the egg.*

> 1 cup cooked brown rice
>
> ¼ cup Pickled Mustard Greens (p. 34)
>
> ¼ cup finely grated carrot
>
> ¼ cup bean sprouts
>
> ¼ cup steamed spinach, squeezed dry
>
> butter
>
> 1 egg
>
> hoisin sauce, optional

Place rice in a deep, single-serving bowl. Arrange vegetables in wedge shapes on top. Melt butter in a small skillet. Add egg and fry sunny-side up. Slide it onto your pile of vegetables and stir with chopsticks or fork, breaking up the yolk. Add hoisin sauce to taste, if desired.

Fiddlehead Tempura

SERVES 4

Crunchy and earthy, fiddleheads are among the first things to appear in the spring markets and the first to disappear. You may have heard that fiddleheads are poisonous. It's not the ferns themselves but bacteria they sometimes harbor that causes symptoms similar to food poisoning. Cooking them thoroughly (they should be a lovely bright green after you boil them) takes care of that.

The key to successful tempura is speed. Have everything else done and on the table before you start, and work as quickly as you can. Tempura tastes best within a minute or two of emerging from the hot oil, so hand each batch to hungry diners before you go back to fry the next.

¼ cup soy sauce

2 tablespoons sesame oil

2 tablespoons freshly squeezed lime juice

1 large clove garlic, grated or pressed through a garlic press

2 tablespoons salt

8 ounces fiddlehead ferns

vegetable oil

1 cup flour, divided

1 tablespoon cornstarch, divided

1½ cups cold seltzer water, divided

Mix together first 4 ingredients (soy sauce through garlic) and set aside. This is the dipping sauce. Bring a large pot of water to a boil and add salt. Boil fiddleheads 5 minutes. Drain and rinse immediately with very cold water to stop cooking. Dry thoroughly.

Pour 3 inches oil into a heavy-bottomed pan and heat to 375 degrees. Only after the oil is fully heated should you start mixing the batter. Whisk together half the flour and half the cornstarch. Stir in half the seltzer water. Drop a handful of ferns into the batter and, using tongs, remove quickly to the hot oil. Don't overcrowd the oil. In a minute or two, the ferns will be crispy but still quite pale. Remove from oil and drain on paper towel–lined plate. Allow oil to return to 375 degrees before starting the next batch. When you've used up the first batch of batter, mix the second half in a clean bowl. Repeat until all the fiddleheads have been fried. Serve hot, with dipping sauce.

Rhubarb Fesenjan

SERVES 4

Fesenjan is a Persian dish traditionally made with pomegranates. Our northern rhubarb has a similar sweet tang that works beautifully as well. This is my adaptation of Joan Nathan's fesenjan in her Jewish Holiday Cookbook. *She uses a whole cut-up chicken, but I prefer my chicken stews without the bones and skin. We serve this with Persian rice, which is parboiled and then steamed and forms a golden, crunchy crust on the bottom.*

> **2 cups finely chopped rhubarb**
>
> **3 cups water, divided**
>
> **1 cup ground walnuts**
>
> **2 tablespoons oil**
>
> **8 boneless, skinless chicken thighs (about 1½ pounds)**
>
> **1 medium onion, finely chopped (about 1 cup)**
>
> **1 tablespoon tomato paste**
>
> **¼ teaspoon salt**
>
> **¼ teaspoon freshly ground black pepper**

Place rhubarb and 2 cups of the water in a small saucepan and bring to a simmer over medium-high heat. Cook 10 minutes, until very soft.

In a dry pan, toast walnuts over medium-high heat until fragrant, about 2 minutes. Stir often to prevent burning.

Pour oil into wide sauté pan with a lid and heat over medium-high heat until shimmering. Carefully place chicken thighs in oil and cook until golden brown, about 2 minutes on each side. (Don't bother to "unroll" the chicken pieces; just leave them as is.) Remove chicken to a plate and set aside.

Reduce heat to medium and add onions. Cook until golden, stirring often to prevent browning. Add toasted walnuts, rhubarb and its cooking water, tomato paste, salt, and pepper, and cook, stirring, about 1 minute. Add remaining cup water and scrape bottom of pan. Place chicken thighs in pan and spoon a little sauce over them (they won't be completely covered). Cover pan and cook at a low simmer 25 minutes.

Remove chicken to serving plate and cover. Simmer sauce uncovered about 10 minutes more to thicken. Taste and add salt and pepper if necessary. Spoon sauce over chicken and serve.

Persian Rice

I learned to make Persian rice—chelo—from our friend Ali, who learned from his mother and grandmother. (Believe it or not, I reduced the amount of salt and oil.) It is drier and fluffier than mosts rice because the starch is rinsed off at the outset and then the rice is parboiled and slowly steamed. Low, slow cooking at the end is essential for developing the prized golden crust, the tahdig.

The amount of rice you use doesn't really matter. Six cups is what comfortably fills my wide-bottomed pan (the only nonstick pan I own, and used almost exclusively for this) about two-thirds full. You can buy a Persian rice maker that will produce a very nice tahdig, but this technique is just as easy.

6 cups long-grain rice, such as basmati

¼ cup salt

¼ cup olive oil

¼ cup plain yogurt

½ cup fresh or dried dill, optional

Wash rice in very cold water, swirling and then draining off the starchy water. Repeat until water is clear, about six times. Bring a large pot of water to a boil. Add salt and rice. Cook 6 minutes. Drain rice and rinse immediately and very well with very cold water, until rice is completely cool. Leave rice to continue to drain.

In a wide-bottomed nonstick saucepan with a tight-fitting lid, swirl together oil and yogurt until it is mixed as well as possible (it won't mix uniformly). Spoon parboiled rice into pan and pat it in smoothly. If using dill, spoon in half the rice, sprinkle dill over top and spoon in remaining rice. Wrap a large, clean kitchen towel around the lid of the pan and knot it securely. Place this tightly on the pan (the layer of towel between the rice and the lid will absorb excess liquid) and place over very low heat for 1½ to 2 hours. The rice is done when a crunchy, golden crust has formed on the bottom. You can check for this by inserting a long wooden spoon along the edge of the rice and lifting gently. To serve, invert over serving platter, crunchy-side up. Serve with stewed vegetables or meat, such as fesenjan.

SWEETS

Honey-Butter Popcorn

Our farmer sells honey made by the bees that pollinate his fields, and I stock the cupboards with it so we have some all year. We bake with it, and we drizzle it on oatmeal, yogurt, pancakes, toast, and peanut butter sandwiches. But sweet-and-salty honey-butter popcorn is our absolute favorite way to enjoy it.

I always melt the butter after *the popcorn has popped. If you pour hot butter on just-popped popcorn, it tends to dissolve.*

> ½ cup popcorn kernels
>
> 3 tablespoons honey
>
> 3 tablespoons butter
>
> 1 teaspoon kosher salt

Pop popcorn kernels however you are inclined to do so. I pop mine on the stove top in a Whirley Pop, which stirs the kernels as they heat.

Pour the popped corn into a large bowl with lots of extra room for stirring. Melt the honey and butter together in the microwave. Alternate a drizzle of honey mixture and a sprinkle of salt over the popcorn, stirring in between.

Rhubarb Syrup, Curd, and Syllabub

I know people who will take a rhubarb stalk, trim it a little, dip it in a bowl of sugar, and chomp. But for most of us, the flavor of raw rhubarb is a bit too intense. It mellows a bit when cooked and, of course, benefits from a little sugar and fat to cut the sourness.

This is a three-part recipe. The syrup is great over ice cream or pancakes or as the base for a soda (mix one part syrup with three parts sparkling water) or cocktail. It's also the first step in making the rhubarb curd, which is lovely spread on crepes or between cake layers, or as a dip for fruit. The curd, in turn, is the base for the delicate syllabub. Easier than a mousse, a syllabub is a flavored whipped cream often served over crumbled cookies.

➤ Rhubarb Syrup

> 2 cups chopped rhubarb
>
> 2 cups sugar
>
> ½ cup honey
>
> 3–4 sprigs thyme

Place all ingredients in a pot and bring to a boil over medium-high heat. Simmer, covered, 15 minutes, until the rhubarb falls apart. Let cool completely, then remove the thyme sprigs. Puree mixture in a standing blender or with a stick blender. Makes 2½ cups.

Variation: Strain out the greenish pulp for a ruby red and more refined syrup.

❧ Rhubarb Curd

> 1 batch Rhubarb Syrup (p. 55), strained to remove green pulp
>
> 6 egg yolks
>
> ½ teaspoon lemon zest
>
> 1 tablespoon lemon juice

Bring syrup to a boil in a small saucepan over medium-high heat and cook, uncovered, until reduced to 1 cup. Let cool in the saucepan to room temperature. Add remaining ingredients and whisk very well.

Cook mixture very slowly over very low heat. Use a double boiler, a glass bowl placed over a pot of simmering water, or the lowest possible setting on your stove top. Stir constantly, being sure to scrape the bottom of the pan. Do not let your curd boil. Remove from heat immediately if you see bubbles. Watch for foam to form on the top of the mixture and for steam to begin to rise. At this point it will have thickened slightly and a candy or probe thermometer will read 160 degrees.

Pour mixture through a mesh strainer, scraping to push it through. Cover and refrigerate for a few hours to allow curd to set. The flavor will deepen overnight.

❧ Rhubarb Syllabub

> 1 cup heavy cream
>
> 2 tablespoons powdered sugar
>
> 1 cup chilled Rhubarb Curd (above)
>
> crumbled shortbread cookies

Combine cream and sugar and whip mixture to stiff peaks. Gently fold in rhubarb curd. Refrigerate for at least 1 hour. Serve with crumbled shortbread cookies.

➤ Rhubarb Cheesecake

SERVES 12

This homey dessert is based on a Russian-style cheesecake. It's not as sweet as an American cheesecake, but it is dense and rich and meant to be served in modest squares, perhaps with a cup of afternoon tea.

> **3 cups chopped rhubarb**
>
> **¾ cup sugar, divided**
>
> **14 graham crackers**
>
> **7 tablespoons butter, melted**
>
> **1 (15-ounce) container whole milk ricotta (about 2 cups)**
>
> **1 cup sour cream or plain yogurt**
>
> **3 eggs, lightly beaten**
>
> **zest of 1 lemon**

Heat oven to 325 degrees. Coat a 7x11-inch glass pan with butter or cooking spray. Toss rhubarb with ½ cup of the sugar and set aside.

Crush graham crackers into a fine sand (a food processor or a blender does this well, but you can also put them in a large plastic bag and bang them with whatever is handy). Mix well with butter and press into bottom of prepared pan. Bake crust 10 minutes.

Mix ricotta and sour cream or yogurt until smooth. Whisk in eggs, remaining ¼ cup sugar, and lemon zest, being sure to fully incorporate the egg whites. Pour ricotta mixture over baked crust. Sprinkle rhubarb over top. Most of it will sink in, but you don't want it fully incorporated. Bake 45 minutes, until set. Refrigerate at least 1 hour before slicing into 2-inch squares.

Chapter Three

EARLY SUMMER (JUNE TO JULY)

As June comes to a close, so do the days of salad every night for dinner. Lettuce doesn't like hot weather, so enjoy the local ones now before they get bitter or disappear from your CSA box or farmers' market altogether.

As the delicate greens finish their season, the heartier greens start to appear. **Spinach** and **kale** are among the most versatile vegetables in the market, and both are great raw or cooked. In **kugels, stir-fries,** and **salads,** you can almost always substitute one where a recipe calls for the other. As the weather heats up even more, spinach will eventually disappear until fall, but kale will keep going strong all summer long.

June's don't-miss treat is one of my favorites: **new potatoes.** The smaller and creamier the better, whether **poached in olive oil** (p. 61), boiled with a **half pound or so of salt** (p. 66), or simply boiled in their delicate skin and coated in good butter. I have been known to make special trips to the farmers' market just for new potatoes.

June also brings **strawberries** and **raspberries.** If you can resist eating them all straight out of the box, throw them on salads and sandwiches. And I always make sure to preserve some for later by making jam and by freezing them. (To freeze, rinse and hull berries. Spread in a single layer on a cookie sheet and place in the freezer. Transfer to bags when completely frozen.)

Warm weather also means it's time to pull out the **grill.** While I often use my griddle pan on the stove top, I love to use the outdoor grill for sliced **zucchini, kohlrabi,** and **radishes.**

Early Summer MENUS

Combinations that highlight the season's best

What's in Season

Arugula	Green Onions	Radishes
Broccoli	Hakurei turnips	Raspberries
Carrots	Kale	Spinach
Chard	Kohlrabi	Strawberries
Collard greens	Lettuce	Turnips
Garlic	Pea shoots	Zucchini
Garlic scapes	Peas	

Spicy Strawberry Jam

Easy as pie? No, easy as jam! Jam making is one of my favorite examples of kitchen chemistry. While water normally boils at 212 degrees, melted sugar actually changes its boiling point as it passes through various stages. The gel stage is eight degrees above water's boiling point, so 220 degrees at sea level. To adjust for your elevation, boil some water and measure the temperature. Add eight degrees to get your gelling point. That is the temperature at which jam becomes jam.

Of course, to make this work, you need a lot of sugar in your recipe—traditionally half the weight of the jam. The easiest thing to do is weigh your berries and use that weight of sugar. If you don't have a kitchen scale, remember that two cups of sugar weighs one pound and a quart of strawberries is roughly one and a half pounds. (Raspberries, by the way, work just as well in this recipe. I don't mind the seeds, so I use the berries whole rather than straining out the seeds.)

The jam will bubble and foam quite a lot as it cooks, so make sure your pot holds about double what you have in strawberries and sugar. A wider pot allows for more evaporation and will make a less runny jam. An experienced jam maker recognizes the gelling point by dripping the jam off a cold spoon (it should fall in sheets rather than drops), but that's not me; I always rely on a probe thermometer.

This recipe is safe for canning if you use canning jars and two-part lids. Process in a hot water bath ten minutes.

2 pounds strawberries, hulled

4 cups sugar

1 small jalapeño pepper, ribs and seeds removed, finely minced

¼ cup freshly squeezed lemon juice

Place berries in a wide saucepan and mash with a potato masher or wooden spoon. Stir in sugar. Add pepper and lemon juice. Bring to a boil over medium-high heat and cook, stirring often, until a candy or probe thermometer reads 220 degrees. Stir down the jam when it bubbles to the top of the pan or remove it from heat if necessary. Keep a close eye on the temperature. It will rise quickly and then hang out between 212 and 219 degrees for quite a while before jumping to 220 degrees. Remove from heat immediately and pour into clean glass jars. The jam will be runny but will set as it cools. Store in refrigerator for up to 1 month. Makes 3 pints.

SALADS AND OTHER SIDES

New Potatoes Poached in Olive Oil

SERVES 4

In our seasonless food culture there are few things that truly cannot be had out of season. Sure, grocery store tomatoes are tasteless in February, but you can buy them if you choose. There are, however, still a few blink-and-you'll-miss-them treats. Some people wait eagerly for ramps or rhubarb. I watch for new potatoes.

The best new potatoes are the size of cherry tomatoes or even smaller, with thin, delicate skin and creamy flesh. They are perfect simply boiled in their skins and tossed hot with butter and chopped herbs. This method is only slightly more complicated and turns out irresistibly crunchy potatoes.

¼ **cup olive oil**

1½ **pounds new potatoes**

1 **cup water**

¼ **cup chopped fresh herbs**

salt to taste

Choose a wide-bottomed pan that easily holds your potatoes in a single layer. Heat olive oil over medium-high heat until shimmering. Add potatoes, water, and herbs and cook, covered, about 20 minutes, until the water boils off and the potatoes have cooked through. Test after about 15 minutes by sliding a knife into one. Very small potatoes will cook more quickly, while larger ones will need more time. If the water starts to boil off too quickly, add more, a few tablespoons at a time. If the potatoes are nearly done and the water is not boiling off, set lid loosely to one side. When a sharp knife easily slips through the potatoes, remove the lid and allow the bottoms of the potatoes to brown in the oil for 5 to 10 minutes, until crispy. Toss with salt to taste and serve immediately.

What's a New Potato?

You may see small potatoes in the grocery store labeled "new" all year long. But true new potatoes are harvested in the early summer when the potato plants are still green, while storage potatoes are harvested in the fall after the plants have died back. New potatoes can be as small as marbles or a little larger than golf balls. Their skin is so delicate you can often rub it off with your fingers—but don't! The skin of new potatoes has a lovely, light, springy flavor, and their flesh is creamy and sweet, rather than starchy or grainy.

Parsley and Onion Salad

SERVES 4

Parsley deserves more starring roles on the table. This salad really showcases its flavor. Sumac—common in Middle Eastern groceries and available elsewhere—adds a warm tartness, but if you can't find it, grate a little bit of lemon zest into the salad.

> 1 large bunch flat-leaf parsley (about 4 ounces), rinsed and dried
>
> 2 bunches green onions (about 20 fat onions), rinsed and dried, roots trimmed

½ teaspoon kosher salt

plenty of freshly ground black pepper

1 teaspoon dried sumac (see head note)

1 tablespoon mellow olive oil

generous squeeze fresh lemon juice

Separate parsley leaves from stems: chop leaves roughly and stems very finely. Slice white parts of onions into slivers; cut green parts into roughly 1-inch slices. Stir together all ingredients and serve.

Pan-Fried Green Beans

SERVES 4

Years ago, the magazine Cook's Illustrated *included a recipe for pan-fried broccoli that immediately became the only way my family would eat broccoli. It seemed a bit complicated at first—with multiple browning and steaming steps—but soon became second nature. I adapted a similar technique for green beans, and they proved to be just as popular as the broccoli. Try these crispy, perfectly seasoned beans, and you'll never boil vegetables again.*

¼ cup water

½ teaspoon kosher salt

½ teaspoon freshly ground black pepper

1 tablespoon olive oil

1 pound green beans, trimmed

Stir together water, salt, and pepper and have ready by the stove. In a wide sauté pan with a lid, heat olive oil over medium-high heat until it shimmers and nearly smokes. Add green beans in a single layer, stir quickly to coat in oil, and then leave alone for 3 to 4 minutes, until they start to brown. Stir in water mixture and immediately cover the pan. Steam 3 minutes and then remove lid and continue cooking until all the water has evaporated. Serve immediately.

Pan-Fried Green Beans with Soy Sauce

Follow directions on p. 63 with these exceptions: Substitute sesame oil for olive oil. Replace half the water with soy sauce. Eliminate salt. Add a teaspoon of sugar to soy sauce mixture.

Pan-Fried Broccoli, adapted from *Cook's Illustrated*

Trim florets from stalk and break into thumb-size pieces. Peel stalk and slice sides so that it is more or less rectangular. Cut on the diagonal into slices. Follow directions above, cooking stalk slices first for 2 minutes before adding florets for 2 minutes. Proceed as above.

Cheesy Kale Chips

Dark greens are good for you, yes—and positively craveable when transformed into crunchy, peppery chips. Both Lacinato and curly kale work well in this recipe. Be sure not to go overboard on the oil, but every bit of the kale needs to be coated; otherwise the result will be limp instead of crisp.

> **1 large bunch kale (about 10 ounces)**
>
> **1 tablespoon oil**
>
> **¼ cup finely grated Parmesan (1 ounce)**
>
> **½ teaspoon kosher salt**
>
> **½ teaspoon freshly ground black pepper or ½ teaspoon red pepper flakes**

Heat oven to 400 degrees. Trim tough center stems from kale and discard (see p. 65). Slice leaves into 1- to 2-inch pieces and place in a large bowl. Pour oil, cheese, and salt and pepper over kale and massage kale well with your hands, making sure every piece is covered, but not dripping, with oil.

Line 2 baking sheets with parchment paper and spread kale in a single layer. Place kale in oven and immediately reduce heat to 250 degrees Bake about 20 minutes, until crisp, stirring kale and turning pans halfway through. Keep an eagle eye toward the end: you want crisp, not brown. When completely cool, store in an airtight container up to 3 days.

Barbecue Kale Chips

Omit Parmesan and pepper. Stir 1 teaspoon pimenton de la vera (smoked Spanish paprika) and ½ teaspoon sugar into the salt before adding.

Radish and Sour Cream Salad

SERVES 4

When I have a bunch of very fresh, peppery radishes, I like to eat them cold, dipped in a tub of sour cream. If I want to get a little fancier for guests, I stir the two together and make this easy salad. A friend grates the radishes, making it a little more like a remoulade, and it is also very good that way, but I enjoy biting into a crisp radish wedge. Stir this together just before serving; the radishes start to give off their liquid and the whole thing gets unpleasantly runny in about an hour.

1 bunch radishes (about 8 ounces)

1 cup sour cream

1 small bunch chives, finely chopped (about ½ cup)

Slice radishes lengthwise into 6 or 8 wedges, depending on size. Mix with sour cream and chives and serve immediately.

Salt Potatoes

SERVES 6–8

Yikes, that's a lot of salt! The salt does more than add a mouth-puckering flavor (although I do like that). It also raises the temperature of the boiling water beyond 212 degrees, which cooks the potatoes more quickly and makes them uniformly fluffy all the way through. For a long time, I thought salt potatoes were a peculiarity of my grandmother's kitchen, but it turns out they are a staple at cookouts and gatherings throughout the area of upstate New York where my parents are from. The salt flats around Syracuse produced much of the salt used in the United States until the early twentieth century.

It's traditional to use new white potatoes about the size of golf balls. But storage potatoes (those harvested in the fall after the potato plants have died back) work, too. The butter is optional but very traditional, and once you've challenged your heart with all that sodium, you might as well throw caution entirely to the wind.

2 quarts water

1 cup table salt or 1½ cups kosher salt

2 pounds whole potatoes

4 tablespoons (½ stick) butter

Add salt to water and bring to a boil. Add potatoes. Boil 20 to 25 minutes, testing for doneness with a knife. Drain potatoes and toss immediately with butter until thoroughly coated.

Steamed Collard Greens with Miso

SERVES 4

In the South, collard greens are traditionally boiled for a very long time, usually with some kind of pork fat. The water in which they boil is a prized treat known as pot liquor. *While I love eating other people's greens cooked this way—when done right, they are melty and smooth—I've never really had the patience to watch over a big pot of boiling water in my hot kitchen. Cooking collard greens quickly is a challenge, however, because they are so tough. At a friend's suggestion I tried steaming them and found them to be delicious, as long as I shred them very finely. Salty, meaty miso is the perfect accompaniment to the slightly bitter greens.*

I've encountered fairly tender collards and very, very tough ones. So taste yours as they steam, as they may need more time. I use a metal steaming basket that fits over a medium saucepan. A bamboo, plastic, or metal steaming insert will work as well. This preparation is tasty hot but also makes a great picnic dish at room temperature.

> 1 large bunch collard greens (about 8 ounces)
>
> 1 tablespoon sesame oil
>
> 2 tablespoons miso paste
>
> 2 tablespoons freshly squeezed lemon juice
>
> 1 teaspoon red pepper flakes

Cut tough center rib out of each collard leaf and discard. Stack leaves and slice crosswise into thin shreds, less than ¼ inch thick. Bring a saucepan with an inch or two of water to boil and place collard greens in basket of steamer over boiling water. Steam, covered, 10 minutes, until tender but still bright green. Shake off any excess water and toss hot greens with sesame oil. Stir together miso paste, lemon juice, and red pepper flakes. Toss with greens.

Gorbunovskiy Salat (Russian Carrot Salad)

This very common salad doesn't actually have a name in Russian beyond "carrot salad," but I learned it from the family I stayed with as an exchange student. They were sure to put it on every festive table, next to the vinegret *and* salat Olivier, *so I have named it after them. It's great on bruschetta or as a sandwich topping (especially on toasted bread). Traditionally, it is made with mayonnaise. Adhering to Russian tastes, this recipe is very garlicky, and you may wish to use a little less. This combination tends to get watery as it sits, so make it shortly before serving.*

> **3 medium carrots, peeled and grated (to yield 1½ cups)**
>
> **¾ cup plain yogurt or mayonnaise (see p. 133)**
>
> **½ teaspoon kosher salt**
>
> **1 small clove garlic, finely grated or pressed through a garlic press**

Stir grated carrots into yogurt or mayonnaise to prevent browning. Stir salt and garlic into carrots. Serve immediately. Makes about 2 cups.

Grilled Zucchini Salad

SERVES 4

Something about dark brown grill marks transforms zucchini from a summertime chore to a treat. And when it's hot off the grill, each slice soaks up the deep, sweet flavor of balsamic vinegar. Some crumbled feta would be a delicious accompaniment, but this salad definitely stands on its own without it.

You can also cook the zucchini outside on the grill, but to avoid sticking, be sure to get it very hot and brush both sides of the zucchini well with olive oil. You may be tempted to use a grill basket or aluminum foil to keep the zucchini from falling to its fiery doom, but unless it sits right on the hot grill, it just won't brown properly.

Use young zucchini, eight inches long or less; they have more tender seeds. If all you have is a great whopping big zucchini, cut it in quarters, slice out the seeds, and then slice diagonally.

> **1–2 tablespoons olive oil**
>
> **4 small zucchini (about 1 pound), trimmed and sliced diagonally into ⅛-inch-thick slices**
>
> **kosher salt**
>
> **freshly ground black pepper**
>
> **1–2 tablespoons good balsamic vinegar**
>
> **6–8 fresh basil leaves, cut into fine shreds**

Brush a grill pan very lightly with olive oil and heat over medium-high heat until shimmering. Working in batches, place zucchini on grill pan and brush very lightly with olive oil. Season generously with salt and pepper. Cook until translucent and grill marks show, about 3 minutes on each side. Remove to a serving plate and sprinkle immediately with balsamic vinegar. Repeat with remaining zucchini, adding grilled zucchini and vinegar to the plate until it's all cooked. Toss gently with basil, using two forks to lift and fold. Serve warm.

Zucchini Rösti

SERVES 4

Watery zucchini rarely gets to taste toasty brown. That's what I love about this rösti, which is based on a Swiss dish traditionally made with potatoes. It's a rather delicate dish, and getting a nice, round, crispy bottom is tricky. Some tips for success: don't skimp on the butter; get the pan nice and hot; press the zucchini down hard (the mixture should be about half an inch thick); to flip it, place a plate upside down on top of the pan and turn the whole thing over. This preparation works well with fresh beets, too. Just cut off the tops and tails, peel them, and grate them (raw), skip the draining step, and proceed.

1 pound zucchini, grated on a box grater (about 2 cups)

½ teaspoon salt

¼ cup flour

2 tablespoons butter

Toss zucchini with salt and let sit in a colander set over a large bowl for about 20 minutes. Squeeze out as much liquid as possible. Transfer to another bowl and toss with flour. Melt butter in a medium, heavy-bottomed skillet and cook until it just starts to brown. Pile zucchini into pan and press down hard with a damp spatula. Cook over medium-high heat, occasionally sliding a spatula around the edges and under the bottom to keep it loose, until the rösti has browned, about 6 minutes. Carefully flip it over onto a plate and slide it back into the pan to brown the other side.

If your rösti doesn't hold together, stir it and serve it proudly as sautéed zucchini.

Kale Salad with Garlic Confit Dressing

SERVES 6

Something magical happens to garlic when you cook it very slowly. The flavor sweetens and deepens, gets a little musky. You can get this flavor in the oven, of course, by roasting a whole head of garlic and squeezing out the cloves. But sometimes you don't want to run the oven for an hour for a single head of garlic. This stove top method makes it easy to keep an eye on your garlic and yields plenty of flavorful oil.

Once you've made the confit, you've got a tasty spread for bruschetta, alongside sea salt or briny olives. You've also got a great addition to a sandwich, a plate of grilled vegetables, and, unforgettably, mashed potatoes. While it's tempting to keep your confit around for a while, you should discard it after a few days in the fridge: garlic in oil is a playground for dangerous anaerobic bacteria.

> ½ cup Garlic Confit, with oil (recipe follows)
>
> ¼ cup freshly squeezed lemon juice
>
> 1 medium bunch curly kale (to yield about 6 cups sliced)
>
> kosher salt and freshly ground black pepper to taste

Puree Garlic Confit and lemon juice in blender. Remove and discard kale stems. Slice leaves into ¼-inch slices (see p. 65). Toss kale with dressing, mixing very well to ensure all surfaces are covered. Season to taste. It's delicious right away and even better the next day.

Garlic Confit

cloves from 1 head garlic, separated and peeled

olive oil to cover (about ½ cup)

Place garlic in your smallest diameter pan. Barely cover with olive oil. Cook on the absolute lowest heat possible for about an hour, until very soft. Do not let the cloves brown at all. Use your nose: if you start to smell browning garlic, remove from heat for a few minutes and allow to cool.

Broccoli Slaw

SERVES 6–8

I love the retro feel of this salad. It's perfect for picnics and, in larger batches, for potlucks. Raisins are traditional, but currants are smaller and not as sweet. The sesame seeds add a little umami flavor, and the sunflower seeds add salt and crunch. I use the mayonnaise recipe on p. 133. If you use commercial mayo, you may decide not to add any sugar.

1 large head broccoli

¼ cup dried currants

2 tablespoons sesame seeds

¼ cup sunflower seeds

2 teaspoons sugar

⅔ cup mayonnaise

salt to taste

Cut florets off stems and chop them very small, no larger than the tip of your thumb. Peel the thickest part of the stem and cut into roughly ¼- to ½-inch pieces. You should have about 4 cups. Mix everything together. It's best if it sits about half an hour before serving.

Don't Discard the Broccoli Stem!

Let's be honest: you probably usually cut off the florets and toss that woody stem into the compost. But you're throwing out my favorite part. Once you've cut off the florets, cut off the thinner branches and slice them thinly. Trim the bottom inch or so off the stem and use a knife to peel off a roughly ⅛- to ¼-inch-thick slice of the skin, working all the way around. You can also place the stem flat on the cutting board and slice off each of 4 sides, to make a rough rectangular prism. Compost the trimmings, sure, but slice the stem on the diagonal or grate it onto a salad. Sadly, if your broccoli stem is hollow inside, it's probably dried out and not very tasty.

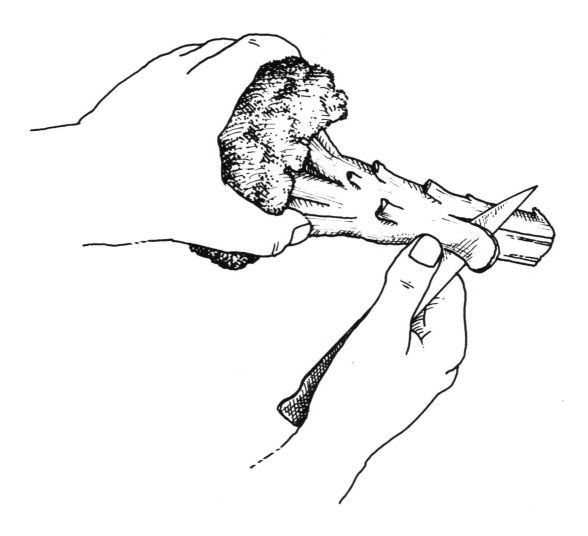

Roasted Scallions with Bagna Cauda

SERVES 6–8

This bold side dish mixes the unexpected sweetness of roasted scallions (also called green onions or spring onions) with the classic Italian anchovy dip. The lemon and red pepper flakes aren't traditional, but I include them to add a little brightness to the sweet and almost smoky tangle of roasted onions.

> 4 bunches scallions (about 24 medium), root ends trimmed
>
> ¼ cup plus 1 teaspoon olive oil
>
> 1 teaspoon anchovy paste
>
> 2 tablespoons freshly squeezed lemon juice
>
> 2 large cloves garlic, peeled and smashed
>
> 1 tablespoon butter
>
> ¾ teaspoon kosher salt
>
> 1 teaspoon red pepper flakes

Heat oven to 350 degrees. Spread scallions in a single layer on a baking sheet. Drizzle 1 teaspoon of olive oil over the scallions and rub in with your hands to be sure they are thoroughly coated. Roast 1 hour, until white parts are quite soft and beginning to brown; some of the leaves will also brown. Turn once or twice during cooking.

Dissolve anchovy paste in lemon juice. Place this mixture and remaining ingredients, including the remaining ¼ cup olive oil, in a small saucepan and turn heat to low. Cook slowly until garlic softens, about 20 minutes. Toss with onions. Serve hot.

Dinner Frittata

SERVES 2–4

When you need to clean out the crisper and get dinner onto plates more or less immediately, a frittata is the perfect solution. Dig out all the leftover vegetables and the last little lump of cheese, and you have what is probably an inimitable dinner. Great frittata vegetables include potatoes (baked, boiled, fried), broccoli, spinach (raw or cooked), green beans, kale, bok choi (raw or cooked), zucchini (raw and grated is great), ramps, pea shoots, asparagus, fennel, eggplant, and onions.

> **2 tablespoons olive oil**
>
> **4 eggs**
>
> **salt and freshly ground black pepper to taste**
>
> **1–2 cups leftover vegetables (see head note), coarsely chopped**
>
> **1–2 ounces cheese, grated or crumbled**

Preheat broiler on low setting. Pour olive oil in a 10-inch, oven-safe, heavy-bottomed skillet and heat over medium-high heat until shimmering. Beat eggs well with salt and pepper. Place the vegetables in the pan and cook about 2 minutes, to give them a chance to brown a little. Pour eggs over vegetables, sprinkle cheese over eggs—don't stir!—and reduce heat to medium-low. Let cook about 10 minutes, until eggs are nearly set, running a silicone spatula underneath occasionally to make sure frittata isn't sticking. When eggs are set on the bottom but just a little runny on top, place under broiler and cook until lightly browned, a couple of minutes, depending on your broiler setting.

Variation: Add 1–2 cups of leftover cooked pasta to brown with the vegetables.

Pea Shoot Risotto

SERVES 4

I love the flavor of shell peas when they've been picked off the vine, shelled between my thumbs, dunked quickly in boiling salty water, and tossed with butter—all within an hour or two. Not being a gardener, I haven't enjoyed this treat very often since my childhood. Pea shoots, with their springy, fresh, sweet, and unmistakably pealike flavor, fill that space for me now. This risotto is like eating a thick bowl of creamy pea soup. This combination is an excellent use for fresh onion if you see it in the markets. Use a mild-flavored vegetable broth or chicken broth or even hot water. A strong broth will overpower the delicate pea shoot flavor.

about 8 cups unsalted vegetable or chicken broth, or water

4 tablespoons (½ stick) butter, divided

½ medium onion, chopped (about ½ cup)

½ teaspoon kosher salt

3 cloves garlic, minced

2 cups arborio or carnaroli rice

1 cup dry white wine

1 fat bunch pea shoots (about 3 cups), roughly chopped

½ cup finely grated Parmesan (2 ounces)

freshly ground black pepper to taste

Bring broth or water to a low simmer and keep it there on the back of the stove. Place 2 tablespoons of the butter with onion and salt in a large, wide-bottomed pan and cook, stirring occasionally, over medium heat until soft and translucent, but not browned, about 10 minutes. Add garlic and cook, stirring frequently, until fragrant, 1 or 2 minutes.

Add rice and increase heat to medium-high. Cook, stirring frequently, until rice has absorbed nearly all of the liquid and the grains start to look translucent around the edges but still have a white spot in the center. Increase heat to high. Add wine and cook, stirring, until rice has absorbed all the liquid. Add broth or water 1 cup at a time, stirring frequently. Add the next cup of liquid when a spatula scraped across the bottom of the pot leaves a dry streak. After the third cup of liquid, add the pea shoots. Continue adding liquid and stirring until rice is cooked al dente. Each grain should be chewy—not crunchy and not mushy—all the way through. At this point, a rich and starchy sauce should have formed in the pot, and the rice will no longer be absorbing the liquid as quickly.

Add one last cup of broth (you may have some left over) and give the risotto a good, vigorous, thorough stir. Remove from heat and add remaining 2 tablespoons butter and Parmesan, stirring vigorously to incorporate. Season with pepper to taste. Serve immediately—on warm plates if you can. Risotto should spread like a very thick soup on the plate and should not sit up in mounds like pilaf.

Fresh Peas: The Clock Is Ticking!

One vegetable I almost always buy frozen is peas. Once peas are picked, they start to lose all their lovely sweetness and go starchy immediately. For that reason, we rarely get peas in our CSA box (but when we do, I shell them and eat them that evening). If I see them in the farmers' market, I ask if they were picked that morning. If the answer is no, I take a pass. I've been disappointed too many times by starchy peas. If you do find freshly picked ones or are lucky enough to have some from your garden, no recipe is needed: give them a quick dunk in boiling water, sprinkle on a little sea salt, and enjoy.

Kale and Beef Stir-Fry

SERVES 4

A stir-fry is one of those dishes that always comes up when someone talks about quick and healthy dinners. I never bought it. All that slicing and prepping, and still the result was soggy, sodden veggies. For years I gave up on stir-fries. And then I learned three tricks: prep work, cooking in batches, and heat—lots of heat.

The key to stir-frying is having absolutely everything ready to go before you start cooking. Don't even turn on the stove until everything is sliced and the sauce is mixed. Then, cook everything in batches small enough to allow them to brown rather than steam. A good rule of thumb is that you should see at least a half inch of space in between individual items. Cook harder items that take longer to cook first.

While I have a wok—a thoughtful wedding gift—stashed away somewhere, I long ago gave up trying to stir-fry in it. The sides just don't get hot enough on a garden-variety home stove. Instead, I use a wide, hard-anodized sauté pan with high, rounded sides. And I let it get hot, much hotter than I do for any other kind of cooking.

I've also learned that, while on TV Chinese cooks keep their stir-fry in constant motion, this technique doesn't work in American home kitchens, where our pans just don't get that hot. Browning means flavor, so I always let meat and tougher vegetables like onions sit for a minute or so at a time.

8 ounces steak (sirloin, top round, and flank steak are good choices)

½ cup soy sauce

4 tablespoons sesame oil, divided

¼ cup freshly squeezed lime juice

1 tablespoon cornstarch

4 cloves garlic, minced

8 ounces kale

2 medium onions, each cut into 8 wedges

About 20 minutes before you start cooking, place steak in the freezer. When you take it out, it will have firmed up enough to allow you to slice it very thinly—as thinly as your knife and skills allow—against the grain.

Mix soy sauce, 1 tablespoon of the sesame oil, lime juice, and cornstarch in a small bowl and set aside. Mix garlic with 1 tablespoon of the sesame oil and set aside. Remove stems from kale and cut leaves in half lengthwise. Stack halves and slice crosswise into 1-inch pieces.

Now you're ready to stir-fry. Heat remaining 2 tablespoons oil in a wide sauté pan over high heat until it just begins to smoke. Add half the beef slices, stir briefly, and allow to cook 1 to 2 minutes, until they start to brown. Stir and cook another minute. Remove to a plate and repeat with the remaining beef.

Allow the pan to heat up again, adding a tiny bit more sesame oil if the pan has lost its sheen. Add onion wedges and give them a brief stir; then allow them to sit a minute or two, until they begin to brown. Stir briefly again and allow to brown a minute or two more. Push onions off to side of pan and add kale. The kale will fill up the pan at first, but keep turning it (kitchen tongs are great for this) until it wilts down, about 2 minutes. Push kale and onion to sides of pan. Add garlic and sesame oil mixture to center and cook, stirring, 1 or 2 minutes, until fragrant.

Now you really need to work quickly. Immediately return beef and any juices to pan. Stir quickly and turn off heat. Immediately add soy sauce mixture and stir, scraping bottom and sides of pan, until sauce has thickened and stir-fry is thoroughly coated, just a few seconds. Serve immediately.

Vegetable Kugel

SERVES 8

The word kugel *is at once nostalgic and heavy. I wanted a springier, zestier, lighter version of this traditional side dish. Lemon and black pepper provide the zest, and very lightly sautéed kale and carrots feel more appropriate to late spring and early summer than to a dark winter dinner. There's very little oil involved, so it's a little lighter as well. Once it's cooled a bit, you can cut this casserole into fairly neat squares.*

zest of 1 large lemon

kosher salt

½ teaspoon freshly ground black pepper

1 tablespoon fresh thyme leaves

1 cup minced onion (about 1 medium)

2 tablespoons olive oil, divided

3 small cloves garlic, minced (about 1 tablespoon)

1 large bunch curly kale, stalks removed, finely chopped (about 8 cups)

3 large carrots, peeled and cut into ¼-inch cubes (about 2 cups)

4 sheets matzoh

4 beaten eggs

Heat oven to 375 degrees. Grease an 8-inch square glass pan. In a small bowl, mash together lemon zest, ½ teaspoon salt, pepper, and thyme leaves with the back of a spoon. Place onions, 1 tablespoon of the olive oil, and a pinch of salt in a large sauté pan and turn the heat to medium. Cook slowly until soft, about 5 to 7 minutes. Add garlic and cook until fragrant, about 1 minute. Add kale, along with another pinch of salt, to onions and cook over medium heat, stirring frequently, until wilted, about 3 to 4 minutes. Remove onions and kale to large bowl. Place remaining tablespoon olive oil and carrots in sauté pan. Cook over medium heat until just starting to soften, about 5 minutes. Remove to bowl with kale mixture and allow to cool.

Hold matzoh quickly under running water and crumble roughly 1-inch pieces into a medium bowl. Stir lemon-pepper mixture into matzoh; then stir in eggs. Combine matzoh and vegetable mixtures. Pour into greased pan and push down lightly with a greased spatula or fingers. Bake 20 minutes. Let sit 10 minutes before cutting and serving.

Minnesota Spring Rolls

Thanks to our long-established Southeast Asian population, Minnesotans can enjoy excellent spring rolls at dozens of restaurants. They're also fun to make at home and adapt well to the flavors of a Minnesota spring: arugula, kohlrabi, pea shoots, and garlic scapes. These nontraditional rolls go especially well with the very nontraditional Creamy Dressing or Goat Cheese Dressing (p. 32 and 30) as a dipping sauce.

1 (14-ounce) block extra-firm tofu

cooking oil

4 ounces thin rice noodles

4 tablespoons rice wine (mirin), divided

1 medium kohlrabi bulb, peeled (see p. 83), cut into matchsticks (see p. 82)

1 large handful pea shoots, gently torn into bite-size pieces

1–2 garlic scapes, cut into ⅛-inch pieces

1 large handful arugula

12 spring roll wrappers

Wrap tofu block in a clean kitchen towel (not terry cloth) and place in a wide, shallow bowl or pan. Place a plate on top of the tofu and a can or other heavy but stable object on top of the plate to press out excess liquid. Let sit for about an hour.

Unwrap tofu and slice into sticks about 2 inches long and ½ inch thick. Pour about ¼ inch of oil into a skillet and heat over medium heat until shimmering. Add tofu in batches, cooking about 4 minutes on each side, until golden brown. Remove to a plate and set aside.

Cook rice noodles according to package directions. Drain and toss with 2 tablespoons of the rice wine. Set aside.

Combine kohlrabi, pea shoots, and garlic scapes and toss with remaining 2 tablespoons rice wine.

Prepare your work surface: set out tofu, rice noodles, vegetables, arugula, spring roll wrappers, and a wide pan of water (big enough to accommodate a spring roll wrapper). Have a plate or tray for the spring rolls nearby, and work on a clean countertop or cutting board. You're going to need to work quickly.

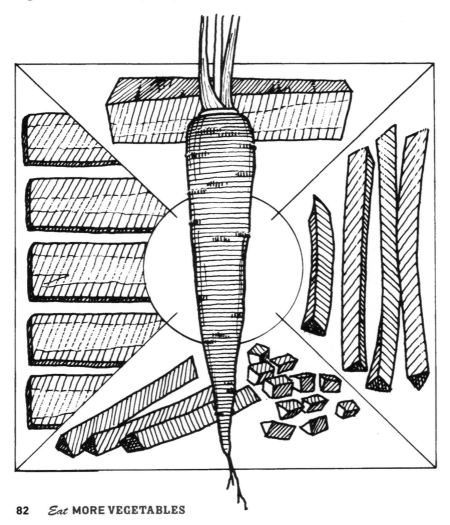

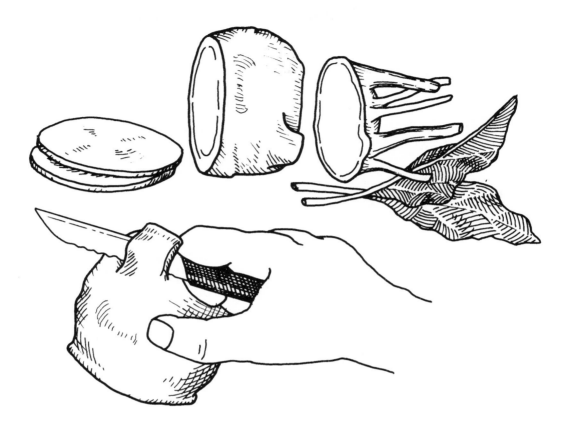

To make each spring roll, hold 1 wrapper in the water for 10 seconds. Remove, shaking off excess water. Place wrapper on your clean work surface. Leaving about an inch from the top and sides of the wrapper, arrange the following in the upper third: 2 leaves of arugula, 2 to 4 pieces of tofu (depending on how you like it), a scant ¼ cup of rice noodles and a scant ¼ cup of vegetables. Fold the top of the circle down and the two sides in. Using your thumbs to keep it tight and smooth, roll the spring roll downward, continuing to fold in the sides as you go. The sticky wrapper will seal itself. Repeat with remaining ingredients. Place spring rolls on serving plate or tray, making sure they don't touch each other. These are best enjoyed right away, but any uneaten rolls can be wrapped tightly in plastic wrap and refrigerated. Makes 12.

Grilled Flank Steak with Charmoula Sauce

SERVES 6–8

> 1 batch Onion-Lemon Marinade (p. 111)
>
> 2 pounds flank steak
>
> Charmoula Sauce (recipe follows)

Use your hands to work marinade into steak; cover and refrigerate 4 to 6 hours (not overnight, as the meat may turn mushy). Drain and brush as much marinade as possible from meat, and grill over high or direct heat for about 6 minutes on each side. Remove to serving plate and let rest about 10 minutes. Slice thinly against the grain and serve with Charmoula Sauce.

Charmoula Sauce

This is my simplified version of the classic Lebanese sauce, which usually includes toasted cumin seeds and other spices. I like this one because I almost always have all the ingredients on hand, and I can make it without much thought while doing a half dozen other things in the kitchen. It also really lets the flavor of the parsley shine. You can use either flat-leaf or curly parsley, although they do have slightly different flavors. I also use this sauce on grilled vegetables, especially eggplants and zucchini. And I always try to have it on the table for our family's taco night.

> 1 cup packed parsley
>
> 1 clove garlic, minced
>
> ¼ cup freshly squeezed lemon juice
>
> ½ teaspoon salt
>
> ½ cup olive oil

Place first 4 ingredients (parsley through salt) in food processor or blender. Pulse several times. With the blade running, pour the olive oil through the feed chute. The sauce will be fairly thin.

Variation: Substitute cilantro for half of the parsley.

SWEETS AND TREATS

Spinach Scones

MAKES 8

Not all treats are sweet. These hearty scones are packed with spinach and the tang of sharp Cheddar, while the cornmeal adds a little flavor and crunch. If you don't have fresh spinach, you can easily substitute frozen: thaw it, squeeze out all the liquid you can, and chop finely. These are best on the day you make them, but the leftovers will freeze beautifully. Reheat in a 400-degree oven.

> oil
>
> 1 pound fresh spinach (see head note), rinsed and dried, stems removed
>
> 3 cups all-purpose flour
>
> ⅓ cup cornmeal
>
> 1 teaspoon salt
>
> 2 teaspoons baking soda
>
> ¼ teaspoon freshly grated nutmeg
>
> ½ teaspoon red pepper flakes
>
> 6 tablespoons (¾ stick) very cold butter, cut into ¼-inch cubes
>
> 1 cup grated sharp white Cheddar (4 ounces)
>
> 1¼ cups buttermilk

Heat oven to 425 degrees. Line 2 baking sheets with parchment paper.

Pour a very thin film of oil into a wide sauté pan and place over medium heat. When oil shimmers, add half of the spinach and cook, turning almost constantly with kitchen tongs, until very wilted, about 3 minutes. Remove to a plate to cool and repeat with remaining spinach. When spinach has cooled to room temperature, use your hands to squeeze all the water you can out of it. Place it on a large cutting board and chop as finely as possible with a large kitchen knife.

While the spinach is cooling, place flour, cornmeal, salt, baking soda, nutmeg, and red pepper flakes in bowl of food processor. Pulse a couple times to combine. Add butter and pulse about 20 times to cut into the flour, until the mixture resembles coarse sand.

Place cheese and cooled, chopped spinach in a large bowl and add flour mixture. Using a rubber spatula, toss the mixture, breaking up any large clumps of spinach, until thoroughly mixed. Add buttermilk and mix thoroughly, but not vigorously, scraping sides.

Turn dough onto a floured surface. Using floured hands, pat into a rectangle about 1 inch high, 5 inches wide, and 14 inches long. Cut into narrow triangles about 2 inches at the base, using a floured knife or bench scraper. The bench scraper is also a good tool for moving the scones from the work surface to the baking sheet. Place scones at least 2 inches apart. Bake 10 to 12 minutes, until just beginning to turn golden brown. Let cool on baking sheet 5 minutes, and then remove to a rack and cool completely.

Annie's Zucchini Bread

MAKES 2 LOAVES

My college roommate gave me this recipe as a wedding present, along with a couple of loaf pans and a good set of measuring spoons. I still use all of them often. I've changed up a couple of things over the years, substituting yogurt for some of the oil and upping the amount of zucchini. Using up zucchini is the whole point of the bread, no? It's also what makes this bread nice and moist.

Definitely grate the zucchini by hand on a box grater rather than lugging out the food processor. Otherwise you'll get long stringy pieces that don't cook evenly. Wrap the second loaf in a double layer of aluminum foil and freeze for up to 3 months. Thaw it in the refrigerator overnight.

½ cup canola or vegetable oil

½ cup plain yogurt

3 eggs

2 cups sugar

3 cups flour

2 teaspoons cinnamon

1 teaspoon ground cloves

1 teaspoon ground cardamom

½ teaspoon baking powder

1 teaspoon baking soda

1 teaspoon salt

3 cups grated zucchini

Heat oven to 350 degrees. Grease and flour 2 (9x5) loaf pans or prepare 18 muffin cups. Beat oil, yogurt, eggs, and sugar. Whisk together dry ingredients (flour through salt) and add to oil mixture. Stir in zucchini.

For loaves: Bake 1 hour until the top is springy and a tester comes out clean. For muffins, bake 25 to 30 minutes, checking for doneness beginning at 15 to 20 minutes.

Variation: Use a mixture of grated carrot and zucchini.

Chapter Four

HIGH SUMMER (MID-JULY TO AUGUST)

One of the cruelest facts of the high summer season is that as soon as those heavy, hot days hit—when standing over a hot stove is the last place we want to be and turning on the oven is unimaginable—that's when our gardens and markets start yielding vegetables that seem to demand to be cooked. One way to get around this truth is to rethink what you can enjoy raw.

Beets and **fennel** are familiar and comforting cooked, but both can be grated or sliced very thinly in a delicious **Shaved Fennel and Beet Salad** (p. 96). **Corn,** when young and very fresh, is also tasty in a raw salad. Raw **zucchini** is a surprising choice for a crudité plate. And just about anything, of course, can be grated into a tasty **slaw.** Cold soups, like **Bloody Mary Gazpacho** (p. 109) and **Šaltibarščiai** (p. 108), are classic summer dishes. You do need to roast or boil the beets for šaltibarščiai, but the gazpacho comes together with nothing but your blender.

While **tomatoes** and **corn** get all the attention this time of year, you want to be sure to give **fennel** some love as well. It is generally only available fresh and locally in August and is fantastic braised or raw. Now is also the time to take advantage of all the plentiful and inexpensive **basil.** Cook with it, savor it, and preserve it for later in big batches of **pesto.**

By late August, the flow of vegetables from your garden, CSA box, or farmers' markets may become overwhelming. It's time to start preserving what you can't keep up with. If canning is too much of a production, make use of your freezer (see "Cleaning Out the Crisper" on p. 22).

High Summer MENUS

Combinations that highlight the season's best

What's in Season

Basil	Cucumbers	Parsley
Beets	Dill	Peas
Broccoli	Eggplant	Peppers
Carrots	Fennel	Potatoes
Chard	Garlic	Summer squash
Cilantro	Green beans	Tomatoes
Collard greens	Kale	Watermelon
Corn	Melon	Zucchini
	Onions	

Beet Hummus

I know not everyone shares my love of beets. I get that the earthy flavor can be just a little too earthy sometimes. But this easy dish may convert some beet skeptics. It's a lovely pink dip, perfect for bruschetta, crackers, or crudités. If you can get your hands on some overwintered beets in the spring, this combination is a fun, bright addition to a spring table, too.

You can make this hummus with very little olive oil and it will be a rough, chunky spread, or you can add the full amount to make it smooth and silky. If you want to lighten it up just a little, reduce the tahini to ¼ cup.

1 medium or 2 small beets (10 ounces)

2 small cloves garlic

½ teaspoon kosher salt

⅓ cup tahini (sesame seed paste)

2–3 tablespoons lemon juice

¼ cup olive oil

Heat oven to 400 degrees. Wrap beets in aluminum foil and roast until very tender, about 75 minutes. The cooking time may vary greatly, and smaller beets will cook faster, so test with a knife after 1 hour.

When beets are just cool enough to touch, slice off ends and rub off skins under cool running water. Chop roughly and place in bowl of food processor with the garlic, salt, tahini, and lemon juice. With blade running, pour the olive oil through the feed chute, stopping when the mixture reaches your desired consistency. Makes 2–3 cups.

Basil and Parsley Pesto

I am a pesto heretic. Classic Ligurian pesto is, of course, made from the tenderest young leaves of fresh basil and woodsy pine nuts. Pesto made that way is delicious—and nearly worth its weight in gold (which is almost what good pine nuts will cost you). Parsley and walnuts bring this classic spread from the realm of luxury into the everyday.

I use a mixture of basil and parsley for two reasons: I enjoy the slightly grassy, slightly tangy parsley flavor, and it helps keep the pesto from turning brown, which basil tends to do as soon as you cut or tear it. This recipe makes a slightly thick, spreadable pesto. If you prefer to drizzle, increase the oil as you pour it through the feed chute until you see the pesto reach the consistency you like.

It's very important that the cheese be grated as finely as possible so that it incorporates smoothly into the pesto. If you don't have a microplane, grate the Parmesan on a regular box grater and then pulse it in the food processor (before you start the pesto) until it is like coarse salt. Pesto freezes very well if you leave out the cheese. Freeze in quarter- to half-cup containers so you only have to thaw out what you need. Stir in the cheese after thawing.

> 2 cups packed fresh basil
>
> 2 cups packed parsley
>
> 2 large cloves garlic, roughly chopped
>
> ⅓ cup roughly chopped walnuts
>
> ½ cup olive oil
>
> ½ cup finely grated Parmesan (2 ounces; see head note)
>
> ¼–½ teaspoon kosher salt

Place basil, parsley, garlic, and walnuts in bowl of food processor. Pulse 5 to 10 times. With blade running, pour the oil through feed chute. Remove mixture to small bowl and stir in Parmesan. Taste and add salt. Makes 1 generous cup.

Eight Tasty Things to Do with Pesto

There are about as many ways to use pesto as there are ways to make it. Keep a small dish of Basil and Parsley Pesto (p. 91), Garlic Scape Pesto (p. 34), Pea Shoot Pesto (p. 46), or Ramp and Mushroom Pesto (p. 33) in the fridge and you can fancy up all kinds of dishes.

1. Toss it with hot pasta. A quarter to a half a cup per pound of pasta yields a decadent creamy sauce. Curly and ridged pasta shapes are particularly good.

2. Spread it on a grilled cheese sandwich.

3. Stir it into mashed potatoes, or top a baked potato.

4. Dollop it onto a frittata or omelet.

5. Top a pizza. In fact, skip the tomato sauce and spread pesto on the crust instead.

6. Spread it on flatbread or bruschetta for an instant appetizer.

7. Pesto chicken: Skip the cheese. Place a half cup of pesto in a plastic freezer bag along with several chicken breasts (boneless or bone in) and freeze until ready to use. Thaw and bake or grill.

8. Stir into soups to thicken and liven them up.

SALADS AND OTHER SIDES

Sweet and Sour Cucumber Salad

SERVES 4

This salad is a summer favorite in our household, and even the youngest members ask for more. It's tart and sweet and refreshing on a hot evening, the perfect counterpoint to grilled meats and also a delicious topping for burgers.

When I use cucumbers from our CSA box, I leave the peel on—I like the crunch and flavor. In other cases, I remove and discard the peel. Commercial cucumber farming uses a lot of pesticides, and grocery store cucumbers are often coated in wax. If I have young, thin cucumbers with small seeds on hand, I don't remove the seeds. But if I have older, fatter ones, I cut them in half lengthwise and scoop out the seeds before slicing.

> 2 tablespoons rice wine (mirin)
>
> 2 tablespoons rice vinegar
>
> 1 tablespoon honey
>
> 1 teaspoon sesame oil (regular or toasted)
>
> 1 teaspoon kosher salt
>
> 1 medium cucumber (see head note), sliced paper thin
>
> 2 large green onions, white and green parts, thinly sliced
>
> 2 generous tablespoons minced fresh dill

Combine rice wine, rice vinegar, honey, sesame oil, and salt in a medium bowl, stirring to dissolve honey. Add cucumbers and onions and stir well. Top with dill. Refrigerate until serving. It's even better on the second day.

Watermelon and Snap Pea Salad

SERVES 4

I'll admit I'm not the biggest fan of watermelon. I find its sweetness a little flat and boring. But with the kick of ginger in this salad, even I slurp up the juices. When the heat and humidity are just too much, this juicy, vitamin-rich salad will perk you right up.

If you don't have a microplane, there are two ways to deal with the ginger: Peel the ginger, then use a vegetable peeler to make very thin slices and mince those finely. Or peel the ginger and then use a grapefruit spoon to scrape against the grain. (Turn it around and try scraping different sides. You'll see the difference.) Do this over a bowl to catch the juices.

1 (1-inch) piece fresh ginger, grated (see head note)

2 tablespoons rice vinegar

1 teaspoon kosher salt

¼ cup finely minced cilantro

2 cups watermelon, cut into matchsticks (2 inches long
and ½ inch thick)

2 large green onions, green parts only, cut into 2-inch lengths

2 cups snap peas, tops and tails removed

In a medium bowl, mix together ginger, rice vinegar, salt, and cilantro. Stir watermelon, onions, and snap peas into dressing. Mix gently but well.

Grape Tomato and Avocado Salad

SERVES 2

I like to make this salad for myself for lunch, but unlike many of the strange things I enjoy eating alone, this one is more than presentable enough for a potluck or party. It's essentially a big bowl of guacamole you can eat with a fork.

1 pint grape tomatoes

1 large ripe avocado

1 tablespoon freshly squeezed lime juice

kosher salt and freshly ground black pepper to taste

Halve grape tomatoes. Slice avocado, scoop out flesh, and cut into ½-inch cubes. Gently stir together all ingredients, taking care not to mash the avocado.

High Summer Chilled Salad

SERVES 6–8

When the heat has driven me away from the stove, I start chopping and look forward to grazing later on a flavorful chilled salad. I especially enjoy using fresh vegetables that we are accustomed to cooking, like fennel, zucchini, and corn. So many variations on this salad are possible, making it ideal for cleaning out the crisper. Some caveats, however: I only use corn if it is very fresh and very young. I try to avoid tomatoes, cucumbers, and other watery vegetables because their texture changes in the fridge. If I substitute basil for the other herbs, I add it just before serving because it tends to brown when cut.

1 fennel bulb, cut into ¼-inch pieces

kernels from 1 ear of very fresh sweet corn (see p. 101)

1 green bell pepper, cut into ¼-inch pieces

1 small, tender zucchini, cut into ¼-inch pieces

1 (16-ounce) can chickpeas, rinsed and drained

8 ounces feta cheese, cut into ½-inch cubes

¼ cup flavorful vinegar (red wine and balsamic are good choices)

¼ cup good olive oil

¼ cup roughly chopped fresh herbs (such as a mixture of oregano and chives)

kosher salt and freshly ground black pepper to taste

Mix everything together. Taste before adding salt and pepper. Refrigerate for at least 1 hour before serving.

Shaved Fennel and Beet Salad

SERVES 4

Crispy, sweet raw beets help carry the intense flavors of fennel, mint, and sumac in this unique summer salad. It's a terrific side dish and an unexpected condiment on hot dogs and burgers. If you can't find sumac, an equal amount of finely grated lemon zest will add a similar tart note. Be sure to mix up this salad ahead of time, to soften the beets and fennel and allow all the flavors to come together. If you don't have a mandoline: For the beets, use a vegetable peeler to shave slices as thinly as possible. Fennel is a little tougher to handle with a vegetable peeler, so use a very sharp knife and a steady hand to cut the thinnest slices you can.

¾ pound beets, tops and stems removed

1 fennel bulb (about 4 ounces)

2 tablespoons neutral-flavored oil (canola)

1 teaspoon minced mint leaves

1 teaspoon dried sumac (see head note)

½ teaspoon kosher salt

2 tablespoons red wine vinegar

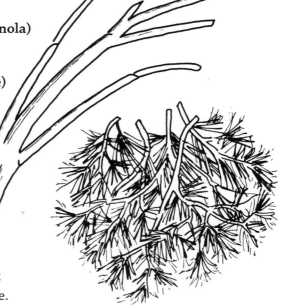

Peel beets by placing cut-side down on a cutting board. Run a sharp knife in stripes down the edges; discard peel. Shave beet in paper-thin slices on a mandoline. Remove fronds from fennel and mince fronds to yield 2 tablespoons; set aside. Shave fennel paper thin on mandoline. Immediately transfer slices to ice water and swish to remove dirt and keep the fennel from yellowing. Remove from water and pat dry. Combine with beets.

Toss beets and fennel with oil, making sure everything is fully coated. Add fennel frond, mint, sumac, salt, and vinegar. Toss well, using kitchen tongs. Let sit at least an hour before serving.

Vinegret (Russian Beet Salad)

SERVES 4

The measure of a Russian cook may lie in how evenly and smoothly she cuts the tiny cubes of meats and vegetables for her salads. I had been struggling to cut perfect cubes with a knife when a Russian friend said, "Why? I just use an egg slicer." Aha! An egg slicer may seem to make ridiculously small cubes but, believe me, the size is authentic for a Russian salad. The kosher dills in the recipe are fermented in a salt brine—rather than pickled in vinegar—and have just the right flavor and texture. Serve as a side dish or part of a smorgasbord of salads, along with small slices of dense rye bread.

>**1 medium beet**
>
>**2 medium carrots**
>
>**2 medium potatoes**
>
>**3 large kosher dill pickles**
>
>**½ medium onion**
>
>**3 tablespoons vegetable oil**
>
>**1 tablespoon red wine vinegar**
>
>**salt to taste**

Wrap the beet in aluminum foil and bake in a 400-degree oven for 40 minutes or until a knife pierces it easily. You may also boil the beet for about the same amount of time. Let cool until easy to handle; then peel and set aside to cool completely.

Boil the carrots and potatoes together, with their skins still on, until cooked through but not soft or floppy, about 20 minutes. Test with a knife to avoid overcooking. Let cool until easy to handle; then peel and set aside to cool completely. (Slicing warm vegetables will result in raggedy cubes.)

Finely chop the beets, carrots, potatoes, pickles, and onion, being careful to cut them all the same size, into about ¼-inch cubes. You may use an egg slicer or a knife, but remember that in proper vinegret, looks count! Stir the oil into the beets and then stir in the remaining ingredients. Serve immediately, before the potatoes turn pink, if you want to impress your guests. Let this salad sit in the fridge overnight if you're making a tasty, solitary lunch.

Pesto, Potato, and Green Bean Salad

SERVES 8

This is a great picnic salad. It's best at room temperature, and the pesto holds up better than mayonnaise on a hot day. Crunchy green beans (be careful not to overcook them) and creamy boiled potatoes are a perfect combination, especially with salty-piquant pesto. Garnish with a little shaved Parmesan if you'd like.

> **1 pound small potatoes (golf ball–size is good), scrubbed and cut into bite-size wedges**
>
> **salt to taste**
>
> **1 pound green beans, trimmed**
>
> **½ cup Basil and Parsley Pesto (p. 91)**

Add potatoes to a very large pot of cold, salted water and bring to a boil. Cook potatoes until tender and easily pierced with a knife, about 20 minutes. Drain and rinse in cool water. Meanwhile, bring a second pot of salted water to a boil and add green beans. Cook about 5 minutes, until crisp tender. Drain and rinse immediately under cold water. Mix potatoes and green beans together and gently stir in pesto.

Roasted Tomato Panzanella

SERVES 8

Roasting the tomatoes and toasting the bread rounds out the flavors of this traditional Italian salad, which can sometimes taste a little sharp and raw. This version is smooth and comforting, with just enough texture. Make this a couple of hours ahead of time for lovely summer picnic fare.

> **2 pounds tomatoes (Romas work well), cored and cut into eighths**
>
> **½ red onion, cut into 1-inch pieces**
>
> **¼ cup olive oil, divided**
>
> **½ teaspoon kosher salt, divided**
>
> **8 ounces crusty bread, cut into 1-inch cubes**
>
> **¼ cup packed fresh basil, thinly sliced**
>
> **2 tablespoons packed fresh oregano leaves**
>
> **2 tablespoons good flavorful vinegar (balsamic)**

Heat oven to 300 degrees. Spread tomatoes and onions in a single layer on a rimmed baking sheet and drizzle with about half the olive oil. Work the oil into the tomatoes and onions a little with your hands. Sprinkle with about half the salt. Roast 2 hours, stirring every half hour or so.

Place bread pieces on a rimmed baking sheet. Drizzle with remaining oil and massage it in a little with your hands. Sprinkle with remaining salt. Toast 30 minutes at 300 degrees, during the last half hour of the tomatoes' cooking time if you like. Let tomatoes and bread cool slightly, about 10 minutes.

In a large bowl, toss tomatoes (scraping all the good gooey stuff off the pan), bread, herbs, and vinegar. Let sit at room temperature 30 minutes to 2 hours so that the flavors mix and the bread softens.

Six Delicious Ways to Eat a Tomato

When the first local tomatoes appear in the markets, it's hard to imagine ever tiring of them. In the early days of the tomato season, you can pick one up and eat it like an apple, maybe sprinkled with a little salt. But the day will come when the tomatoes stack up on the counter. Here are some ways to keep the love alive.

1. *Pan con tomate:* Toast some good, crusty bread. While it's still hot, rub the surface first with a clove of garlic and then with the cut side of a tomato. Drizzle with really fruity olive oil and sprinkle with coarse salt.

2. *Tomatoes and eggs:* Slice a tomato into wedges and fry them quickly in as much olive oil as you dare. Push them to the side and fry an egg in the same pan until the white is frizzled and the yolk just barely set.

3. *Chill it:* While a sun-warmed tomato is many people's idea of heaven, Japanese connoisseurs enjoy firm, chilled tomatoes. Try it this way for a change.

4. *Caprese spears:* a classic. Spike a cherry tomato or tomato slice on a toothpick and add a basil leaf and a small mozzarella ball. Drizzle with excellent olive oil.

5. *Sweet and sour:* Toss coarsely chopped tomatoes with a sprinkle of sugar, salt, and balsamic vinegar.

6. *Fat tomato sandwich:* Slice a big tomato thicker than you would a holiday ham and sandwich it between two pieces of toast liberally spread with good mayo. Making your own mayo, it turns out, is so easy that I recommend whipping up a small batch when you need it, rather than keeping a big jar in the fridge (see p. 133).

Corn Pudding

SERVES 4

While this isn't my grandmother's recipe for corn pudding, it is an homage to Sunday dinners at her table. This pudding sets up like a cheesy soufflé but should still be soft and creamy in the middle. While the size of the pan you use isn't absolutely crucial, if you choose a shallower pan the pudding will cook much more quickly and be a little stiffer.

When you cut the kernels off the corn cobs, be sure to "milk" the cobs. First slice off kernels, then run the dull edge of the knife down the cut surface to dislodge the bases of the kernels and the remaining juices. If your corn isn't very fresh and very young, cook it for five minutes in boiling water first to make it tender.

2 tablespoons butter

½ medium onion, minced

1 teaspoon kosher salt

½ jalapeño pepper, seeds and ribs removed, thinly sliced, optional

3 cups corn kernels (about 3 ears; see head note)

4 eggs, separated

½ cup grated cheese (2 ounces; fontina is a good choice)

Heat oven to 350 degrees. Grease a 1½-quart soufflé pan or other deep baking dish. Melt butter in saucepan over medium heat. Soften onions in but-ter, with salt, about 5 minutes. Do not brown. Add jalapeño if using, and cook until fragrant, about 1 minute. Stir in kernels. Remove from heat and let cool to room temperature.

Beat egg whites to stiff peaks. In a separate bowl, beat egg yolks until smooth. Stir cooled corn mixture and cheese into egg yolks. Fold in beaten egg whites. Slide into prepared pan. Bake 45 minutes, until firmly set and barely golden brown on top. A toothpick will not come out clean, but the top should not jiggle.

Braised Fennel

SERVES 4

Too often relegated to soups, fennel rarely gets a chance to shine. This dish showcases fennel in all its licorice-y glory. The sweet, faintly grassy tarragon intensifies the anise notes in the fennel, and allowing it to brown before it steams adds another layer of flavor. This recipe makes a modest side dish for four but scales easily. For true fennel lovers, you'll want about one fennel bulb per person.

2 large fennel bulbs (about 1 pound)

1 tablespoon olive oil

1 tablespoon dried tarragon

salt and freshly ground black pepper to taste

½ cup water

Remove fronds from fennel bulbs and reserve for another use (see Fennel Walnut Pasta, p. 115). Slice off root end of the bulbs and discard. Slice bulb lengthwise into ⅛-inch-thick slices. Swish slices quickly in ice water to clean and prevent browning. Heat a thin film of olive oil in a large sauté pan over medium-high heat until shimmering. Add fennel, tarragon, and salt and pepper. Stir quickly to coat, spread the slices into an even layer in the pan, and then allow the bottom slices to brown, about 4 minutes. Give the fennel another stir, add water, quickly cover, and reduce heat to medium-low. Cook until the water has evaporated and the fennel is golden brown throughout.

Bacon-Wrapped Tomatoes

Bacon cooks up salty and crispy; tomatoes cook up sweet and gooey. Together they make the perfect little bites. These are a little fiddly, because you need the toothpicks to hold everything together at first and then you pull them out to cook the remaining sides. It's totally worth it, however, and a great party trick. Do not pop one into your mouth straight out of the pan: they are nearly lethal when hot.

grape tomatoes

thinly sliced bacon

oil

Wrap a half slice of bacon around each tomato and secure with a toothpick poked all the way through. Pour a thin film of oil in a skillet and set over medium-high heat. Place the tomato skewers in the pan and cook on each more-or-less flat side until brown and crispy. The bacon should now be sealed around the tomato. Remove the skewers from the pan and pull out the toothpicks. Return to pan and cook on remaining sides until brown and crispy. (Kitchen tongs are invaluable for this task.) Let cool 10 minutes before serving.

Grilled Corn with Chili-Lime-Chive Butter

Lime and chili powder are traditional toppings for corn on the cob—called elote in Mexico—and you'll understand why as soon as you take a bite. Heat and tang are just what sweet corn needs. Although you don't find corn in traditional Indian cuisine, it also relies on melding sweet and savory flavors, which inspired the second choice of toppings. The flavor will deepen overnight, so make the butter in advance if you can.

Soak sweet corn still in its husk in cool water for about 30 minutes. Drain corn and wipe off excess moisture. Grill over high or direct heat about 30 minutes, turning at least once during cooking. Some of the husks will become quite charred, which will only add flavor to the corn. Serve with pats of compound butter (recipes follow).

Chili-Lime-Chive Compound Butter

¼ cup minced chives

¼ cup tightly packed lime zest (from at least 4 medium limes)

2 teaspoons chili powder

½ teaspoon kosher salt

½ cup (1 stick) unsalted butter, at room temperature

Stir together first 4 ingredients (chives through salt) in a small bowl. Use a spatula to smash and scrape the softened butter into the mixture. Scoop onto a 6x6-inch sheet of waxed paper, forming a row about 5 to 6 inches long. Roll 1 side of the paper along the long side of the row, and gently work the butter into a neat cylinder encased in paper. Twist the ends like an English Christmas cracker and refrigerate until very firm, at least 2 hours.

Before serving, slice the log into 8 neat disks and arrange on a plate for everyone to slather on their own corn.

Indian-Spiced Compound Butter

Asafetida can be found in Indian or other ethnic groceries. Its flavor is like nothing else—a combination of maple syrup and leeks. If you can't find it, I recommend leaving it out rather than making a substitution.

2 teaspoons chili powder

½ teaspoon ground cumin

½ teaspoon ground coriander

½ teaspoon asafetida

½ cup (1 stick) unsalted butter, at room temperature

Follow instructions for Chili-Lime-Chive Compound Butter.

Sautéed Sweet Corn with Dill

SERVES 4

This savory side dish is nearly as quick and easy to put on the table as is a plate of boiled corn on the cob. Dill is an unexpected addition, but it really sings next to the sweetness of the corn and the onion.

> 2 tablespoons butter
>
> 1 medium onion, chopped
>
> ½ teaspoon salt
>
> 4 cups corn kernels (from 4 large ears)
>
> ¼ cup minced fresh dill

Place butter, onion, and salt in a wide sauté pan and cook over medium heat until onion is soft but not thoroughly translucent and definitely not brown, about 5 minutes. Add corn and dill and cook, stirring occasionally, 3 to 4 minutes. Remove from heat while corn still retains much of its crunch.

Eggplant Fries

SERVES 4

After you lift these eggplant fries out of the oil, the window between tongue-searingly hot and already limp is very brief—just minutes, really. But during that window, they are crisp and light on the outside and magically gooey and creamy on the inside. After they've cooled and softened a bit, they're still quite tasty. I recommend wrapping them in a pita or tortilla with hummus and greens and a little extra paprika or tossing them in a salad of late summer greens.

Be sure to use a thermometer you trust; if the oil isn't hot enough, these little sponges will soak it all up and not crisp on the outside. You can remove the skin, but I like to leave it on for a little extra eggplanty flavor.

oil

1 cup flour

1 teaspoon salt

2 teaspoons dried oregano

1 teaspoon sweet paprika

¼ teaspoon chili powder

½ teaspoon freshly ground black pepper

1 pound eggplant, cut into matchsticks (3–4 inches long and ½ inch thick)

kosher salt to taste

Pour at least 3 inches of oil into a heavy-bottomed saucepan. Heat oil to 375 degrees, monitoring the temperature with a candy or probe thermometer. Meanwhile, stir together flour and spices and toss with eggplant. Working in small batches (about a quarter of the eggplant at a time), carefully drop eggplant sticks into hot oil. Keeping a close eye on the temperature, cook 4 minutes, until quite brown. Remove to a paper towel–lined plate and sprinkle immediately with kosher salt. Bring oil back up to temperature and repeat with remaining eggplant.

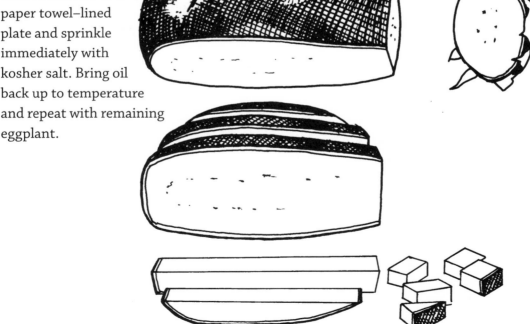

Soupe au Pistou

SERVES 6–8

I look forward to this soup all year long and make it as soon as we have basil, potatoes, and green beans in the CSA box. It's both filling and light, packed with vegetables and flavor—the perfect dinner on a warm evening.

All the vegetable amounts in this recipe are approximate and can easily vary with what you've got and what you like. The pistou—*a French pesto—is* de rigeur, *and for me it just isn't the same without green beans. The potatoes and bread give the soup a little body; other recipes include white beans or ver-micelli for this purpose. A cup of fresh corn kernels is a welcome addition.*

For the pistou:

4 cloves garlic

½ cup packed chopped fresh basil

¼ cup olive oil

1 small tomato

½ cup finely grated Parmesan (2 ounces; with a microplane is best)

Place garlic and basil in bowl of food processor and, with blade running, pour olive oil down feed tube. Add tomato and pulse until blended. Scrape mixture into a small bowl and stir in Parmesan. Set aside.

For the soup:

2 tablespoons olive oil

2 cups finely chopped carrots

2 cups finely chopped onions

2 cups finely chopped green bell peppers

2 cups peeled and finely chopped potatoes

2 cups green beans, cut into 1-inch pieces

1 slice fresh or stale bread, crust removed, crumbled

salt and pepper to taste

Place the olive oil, carrots, onions, peppers, and potatoes in a large heavy pot. Cook over medium heat until just softened but not brown, about 10 minutes. Add green beans and bread, cover with water by about 3 inches, and bring to a simmer. Cook for 15 to 20 minutes, until potatoes are soft but green beans are still just slightly crunchy. Using a fork, mash some of the potatoes against the side of the pot and stir. Add salt and pepper to taste. Serve in bowls with a dollop of pistou on top.

Šaltibarščiai (Lithuanian Cold Beet Soup)

SERVES 4

Rosy pink and refreshing, cold beet soup is a summertime classic in the Baltics, and there are as many versions as there are family summer houses with beet patches. I prefer this rendition, with kefir as the creamy base. Others use the beet cooking water as the broth, with just a little sour cream stirred in.

A plate of boiled potatoes and eggs for each person is absolutely necessary. You could, of course, get fancy and chop the eggs and potatoes for a garnish, but I prefer to have a little bite of potato, a little slurp of soup, a little bite of egg, a little slurp of soup . . .

1 pound beets

1 medium cucumber, cut into ¼-inch cubes

4 cups kefir or buttermilk

salt to taste

sour cream

chopped green onions, dill, or chives

hard-cooked eggs

boiled potatoes

Boil beets in enough water to cover for about an hour. The cooking time will vary according to the size of your beets; check for doneness by piercing with a knife. Remove beets and reserve 1 cup of the cooking water. When cool enough to handle, peel beets under cool running water. Refrigerate until completely cool.

Grate beets on a box grater. Combine beets, reserved cooking water, cucumber, and kefir or buttermilk, stirring to mix, and refrigerate for at least an hour. Add salt to taste.

Serve with a dollop of sour cream and a sprinkling of chopped green onions, dill, or chives, alongside a plate of boiled eggs and potatoes cut into wedges.

Bloody Mary Gazpacho

SERVES 6–8

There are lots of directions you could go when making gazpacho: The classic Spanish version includes bell peppers and garlic. You could make it Italian with basil or Latin with chili peppers. I prefer the tang and heat of a good old American bloody Mary. My version is a little pulpy rather than chunky and best enjoyed icy cold. It keeps well in the refrigerator without separating.

1 slice soft white bread, crust removed, crumbled

2 pounds tomatoes, cored and roughly chopped

½ medium red onion, grated

2 stalks celery, roughly chopped

2 tablespoons Worcestershire sauce

1 tablespoon anchovy paste

1 teaspoon sriracha chili sauce

¼ cup freshly squeezed lemon juice

1 teaspoon kosher salt

¼ cup olive oil

Place all ingredients in a blender and puree until very smooth. Refrigerate at least 1 hour, and serve very cold.

Creamy Bloody Mary Gazpacho

Leave out the bread and strain the mixture after pureeing. Stir 1 cup vodka into 4 cups gazpacho.

MOSTLY MAIN DISHES

Corn and Zucchini Fritters

SERVES 4

Light, fluffy, and crispy, these fritters were inspired by my husband's Grandma Lusia's Latkes (p. 178). I love the combination of hot and crunchy with the sweet, tender corn. If your corn is young and fresh, it will be sweet and delicious right off the cob. But if your corn is more than a day or two away from the farm or if it's the last corn of the season, you'll want to boil it about five minutes before cutting off the kernels. Be sure the corn is cool before mixing it with the other ingredients.

2 cups grated zucchini

1 teaspoon kosher salt

oil

kernels from 2 ears corn

4 eggs, separated

1 cup matzoh meal or dry, unseasoned bread crumbs

freshly ground black pepper to taste

Toss zucchini with salt and let sit in a colander for about 15 minutes. Squeeze out and discard liquid. Heat ½ inch oil in a wide pan to 375 degrees. You want to be able to start frying as soon as you mix the batter.

Combine zucchini with corn, egg yolks, matzoh or bread crumbs, and pepper. Whip egg whites to stiff peaks and stir 1 cup egg whites into zucchini mixture to lighten it. Plop remainder of whites on top and fold them in gently, inserting spatula sideways into the center and scraping along the bottom from the middle to the sides.

Drop ¼ cup batter into the hot oil at a time; it should spread and then puff. Cook about 3 minutes on each side, until quite brown. Repeat with remaining batter. Serve hot.

You can freeze the fritters by placing them on a tray in a single layer and then transferring them to a plastic bag when frozen. Reheat in a single layer in a 350-degree oven.

Onion-Lemon Marinated Chicken Skewers

SERVES 4

This recipe came to me after years of throwing an onion in with my standard lemon juice and olive oil marinade. I started to wonder why I bothered. I wanted to really taste the onion in the finished dish. So I dispensed with nearly all the liquid so that the onion itself could do the work of flavoring and tenderizing the chicken. The method looks a little crude, and anyone watching you prepare it might think you've gone a little addlepated in the summer heat. But they won't argue after they've tasted it.

You can use metal or wooden skewers for this recipe. If you use wooden ones, at least an hour before cooking, place them in a sink or shallow dish to soak, weighting down if necessary.

2 large onions, peeled and quartered or cut into eighths

2 large lemons, unpeeled and quartered or cut into eighths

¾ cup olive oil

1 teaspoon kosher salt

4 chicken breasts (about 1½ pounds), cut into 1-inch cubes

Make marinade the night before. Place onions and lemons in bowl of food processor or blender with olive oil and salt. (Some blenders with a good ice function can handle this step; others cannot.) Pulse until onions and lemons are very finely chopped and the mixture is thick and pulpy, scraping down the sides as needed. In a glass bowl, stir chicken and marinade together, using your hands to work marinade into chicken. Cover and refrigerate 8 hours or overnight.

Remove chicken pieces from marinade (discard marinade) and scrape off as much excess as possible. Thread tightly onto 6 skewers. Grill over medium-high heat (gas grill) or direct heat (coals) about 10 minutes, covered, turning once. Be sure to use a knife to check for doneness all the way through, or cook to an internal temperature of 180 degrees.

Vegetable Bread Pudding

SERVES 6–8

This savory dish is great for either breakfast or dinner. It comes together quickly and stands on its own without a lot of fussing with side dishes. It also works very well as a vegetarian dish: just leave out the sausage and increase the salt a bit to make up for it. Check it early to be sure it doesn't dry out. The tops of the bread cubes—crusty bread works best—will get crunchy, but the inside should stay moist.

8 ounces ground Italian sausage

1 cup grated zucchini

¼ teaspoon salt

1 cup corn kernels (from 1 ear corn)

1 cup chopped tomato (about 3 small Romas)

¼ cup finely chopped parsley

¼ cup finely chopped chives

2 medium cloves garlic, pressed through a garlic press or grated on a microplane

½ teaspoon freshly ground black pepper

4 cups (1-inch) bread cubes

4 eggs, lightly beaten

1 cup no-sodium chicken or vegetable broth

Grease an 7x11-inch or other shallow 2-quart pan. Cook sausage meat until brown in a wide pan over medium heat. Set aside. Toss zucchini with salt and let sit in a colander about 15 minutes. Squeeze out and discard liquid.

Mix sausage, zucchini, corn, tomato, parsley, chives, garlic, and pepper. Add bread cubes. Combine eggs and broth and mix thoroughly. Stir into vegetable mixture. Pour into pan and press down firmly. Cover and refrigerate 8 hours or overnight.

Bake 35 to 40 minutes in a 350-degree oven. Let sit 5 to 10 minutes before serving.

Shakshuka

SERVES 4

Shakshuka *means "all mixed up." It's a popular Israeli dish my kids learned to cook at camp one summer. They came home begging to make it, which isn't the reaction I would have predicted for a big pot of vegetables. But, hey, eggs and tomatoes? I could get on board with that. The camp variation called for scrambling the eggs lightly into the tomato sauce, but I think there's nothing better than a perfectly poached egg yolk.*

Note: To prepare the tomatoes, bring a pot of water to boil and submerge tomatoes until you see the skin crack, about one minute. Let cool slightly, remove peel, and cut out core.

2 tablespoons olive oil

1 medium onion, finely chopped

1 medium green bell pepper, finely chopped

1 Anaheim or jalapeño pepper, seeds and ribs removed, finely chopped, optional

1 teaspoon salt, plus more to taste

4 cloves garlic, minced or grated on a microplane

4 medium tomatoes, peeled and chopped (see head note)

½ cup water

4–6 eggs

4 ounces crumbled feta

2–4 green onions, coarsely chopped

Place olive oil, onion, green pepper, and Anaheim or jalapeño, if using, in a saucepan large enough to hold all the eggs side by side. Sprinkle with salt and cook over medium-low heat until soft but not brown, about 10 minutes. Add garlic and cook, stirring, until fragrant, about 1 minute. Stir in tomatoes and water and increase heat to bring mixture to a simmer. Simmer until slightly thickened, about 15 minutes. Crack eggs gently into mixture, cover, reduce heat to low, and poach until the whites are set, about 5 minutes. Sprinkle with feta and onions for serving.

Fennel Walnut Pasta

SERVES 4

Here's what you can do with the fennel fronds, after you braise the bulbs (p. 102). The two dishes together make a nice meal. The toasted walnuts add a little crunch, and finishing the pasta in the sauté pan with the cooking water makes a light, silky sauce.

> **fennel fronds from 1–2 bulbs**
>
> **1 pound bowtie pasta**
>
> **1 tablespoon olive oil**
>
> **1 cup chopped walnuts, toasted**
>
> **salt and freshly ground black pepper to taste**

Remove the thin, soft fennel fronds and discard the thick, tough stems. Chop fronds roughly to make about 1 cup, packed.

Bring a large pot of water to a boil and add a generous amount of salt. Cook pasta al dente according to package instructions. Before draining, reserve 1 cup cooking water.

Heat olive oil over medium heat in a sauté pan large enough to hold cooked pasta. Add chopped fennel fronds and heat through. Toss with cooked pasta, reserved cooking water, toasted walnuts, salt, and pepper. Cook until pasta has absorbed remaining water.

Eggplant Salad

SERVES 8

To me, late summer tastes like eggplant and tomatoes. This hearty cooked salad brings these two good friends together, along with a supporting cast of other summer favorites: green peppers, onions, and basil. It's a lot like a rata-touille, that rustic classic of southern France, but, frankly, even more relaxed and easier to make. This dish is delicious warm, right out of the pot, and even better at room temperature, after it has sat in the fridge overnight, letting the flavors meld.

1 large eggplant, cut into ½-inch cubes (about 6 cups)

1 teaspoon kosher salt

¼ cup tomato paste

¼ cup white vinegar

1 teaspoon sugar

3 cloves garlic, pressed through a garlic press or grated on a microplane

2 tablespoons oil, divided

1 medium onion, chopped

1 medium green bell pepper, chopped

1 large bunch green onions (about 10), chopped

2 cups chopped Roma tomatoes

1 cup chopped kalamata olives

10 leaves fresh basil, thinly sliced

freshly ground black pepper to taste

Place eggplant in a colander and sprinkle with salt. Allow to sit about half an hour and discard any liquid. Mix tomato paste, vinegar, and sugar in a small bowl. Stir in garlic.

Heat 1 tablespoon of the oil in a wide sauté pan over medium-high heat. Add eggplant and cook, stirring occasionally, until brown, about

5 minutes. It should remain fairly firm. Remove eggplant from pan and set aside. Heat remaining tablespoon oil over medium-high heat and add onion, green pepper, and green onions. Cook, stirring occasionally, until the pepper turns a brighter green and the onion just barely browns. Try not to let them soften too much. Stir in tomatoes and cook about 2 minutes. Stir in eggplant, tomato paste mixture, and olives. Cover and cook over low heat about 20 minutes. Stir in basil and pepper. Taste and adjust for salt. Serve warm or at room temperature.

Grilled Eggplant with Roasted Red Pepper

SERVES 4

Eggplants and red peppers are good companions, and they both love the grill. This light entrée is pretty on the table and tasty both hot and at room temperature. You may be tempted to skip the anchovy paste, but please don't! Its flavor here is meaty and deep, rather than fishy.

> **2 large red bell peppers**
>
> **1 large eggplant**
>
> **1 teaspoon kosher salt, divided**
>
> **3 tablespoons olive oil, divided**
>
> **1 tablespoon freshly squeezed lemon juice**
>
> **1 tablespoon anchovy paste**
>
> **2 tablespoons minced garlic (about 2 large cloves)**
>
> **8–10 leaves fresh basil, thinly sliced, plus more for garnish**

Preheat grill on high for several minutes. With the lid down, grill peppers about 15 to 20 minutes, turning several times, until blistered all over. Place peppers in a mostly airtight container (a glass bowl with a lid or plate on top works well) for about half an hour, until cool enough to touch.

While the peppers are on the grill, slice eggplant ½-inch thick, place in a single layer on a platter or plate, and sprinkle about ½ teaspoon salt over them. Let sit for about 20 to 30 minutes, then pat dry.

Brush eggplant on both sides with about 1 tablespoon of the oil. Grill about 5 minutes on each side, allowing them to become a little translucent and droopy; they'll have much more flavor than when they're still whitish and dry.

While the eggplants are on the grill, peel the peppers. Use your fingers to pull out the stem and seeds, holding the peppers over a mixing bowl to catch as much of the juices as possible. Rub the pepper skin off with your fingers. Discard stem, seeds, and skin. Slice peppers in bite-size pieces and mix with juices, remaining 2 tablespoons olive oil, lemon juice, anchovy paste, garlic, basil, and remaining ½ teaspoon salt. Arrange eggplant on a serving platter and spoon peppers on top. Garnish with a little more fresh basil.

SWEETS AND TREATS

Cucumber Lassi

MAKES 2 TALL DRINKS

This refreshing summer drink isn't sweet, but it is a treat. On hot days I crave salty and tart flavors like this. A lassi is a traditional Indian yogurt drink that is sometimes sweet and sometimes savory. A pinch of cumin, coriander, or black pepper would also be a great addition here.

> **1 medium cucumber, peeled, quartered lengthwise, seeded, roughly chopped**
>
> **1 cup plain yogurt**
>
> **1 scant cup water**

½ teaspoon kosher salt

6–8 small mint leaves

1 cup ice

Place first 5 ingredients (cucumber through mint) in a blender and puree. Add ice and pulse to crush.

Summer Squash Jam

When you're drowning in summer squash and zucchini, you need to explore both savory and sweet options to keep up with Mother Nature. Zucchini bread is great, of course, but here is something a little different. It's sweet and tart and, yes, a little squashy. But if you never tell anyone what your secret ingredient is, they may never guess. While zucchini will work in this recipe, it yields a rather unappetizing color. This recipe is not tested for home canning, but it freezes very well.

2 pounds summer squash

¼ cup water

zest of 4 lemons

1 cup lemon juice

1 (1¾-ounce) package pectin

4 cups sugar

If your squash is bigger and older, peel it and quarter it lengthwise so you can slice out the seeds and the soft matter surrounding them; then grate the remaining flesh. Otherwise, just grate smaller squash skin, seeds, and all on a box grater. In a saucepan, cook the squash with the water at a simmer for about an hour, until it has become quite soupy. Stir in the zest, lemon juice, and pectin. Bring mixture to a full boil and stir in sugar. Continue to boil 1 minute. Pour into 4 clean pint jars and refrigerate. Once jam has set, store in the refrigerator for up to 2 weeks or freezer for up to 3 months. Makes about 8 cups.

Gingery Grilled Watermelon

Watermelon's simple sweetness is great for dessert, but on the grill its flavor becomes deeper and more sophisticated, making it ready for cocktail hour or appetizers.

> 1 (2- to 3-inch) piece fresh ginger, peeled and grated
>
> 3 tablespoons sesame oil
>
> 8–10 (1-inch-thick) triangles watermelon
>
> coarse salt

Mix ginger with sesame oil on a large plate, spreading out mixture to cover. Rub both sides of each watermelon slice in mixture. Grill watermelon on high, uncovered, 3 to 5 minutes per side. It will start to sweat and dry out just a little. Be sure to wait long enough to make nice brown grill marks on each side. Remove to a serving platter and sprinkle lightly with coarse salt. Serve warm.

Sweet Corn Ice Cream with Chili-Lime Salt

Corn has been bringing sweetness to side dishes for generations: I'm thinking of my grandmother's custardy creamed corn, which always made me feel like I was getting away with something when I put a scoop next to my roast beef at Sunday dinner. So why not a corn dessert? This sweet corn ice cream is very rich, slightly tangy, and delicately corn flavored.

Cream cheese is a handy cheat when you want to make a creamy ice cream but don't want the bother of boiling a custard. One blitz in the blender, and you're ready to go. Don't, however, be tempted to skip the overnight chilling step. You want the mixture to be very cold when it hits your ice cream maker.

If you can't get very fresh, young corn, boil it for about five minutes before using. The Chili-Lime Salt is a bold, tangy touch, inspired by elote, *a favorite Mexican preparation of corn with chili powder, lime, and crema. A light sprinkling of fresh lime zest is very tasty as well.*

2 ears very fresh sweet corn

8 ounces cream cheese

1½ cups half-and-half

1 tablespoon freshly squeezed lime juice

¾ cup sugar

⅛ teaspoon salt

Chili-Lime Salt (recipe follows)

Cut kernels from cobs (you should have about 2 cups) and "milk" the ears (see p. 101), using a bowl to catch all the corn and liquid released. Place first 6 ingredients (corn through salt) in blender and puree. Chill mixture overnight (it will separate in the refrigerator; just stir it up). Place in your ice cream maker and freeze as directed. If you don't have an ice cream maker, chill overnight and then freeze mixture in ice cube trays. Pulse cubes in bowl of food processor. The texture will be more like a flaky granita, but it will still be tasty. Sprinkle judiciously with Chili-Lime Salt before serving.

Chili-Lime Salt

2 tablespoons lime zest

½ teaspoon kosher salt

½ teaspoon chili powder

Mix ingredients well. Keep this combination on hand to spruce up store-bought vanilla ice cream as well.

Peak Corn

Is your sweet corn fresh enough? Break off a kernel with your thumb and try it. If you want to keep eating the whole cob, then it is fresh enough. Generally speaking, if your corn wasn't picked that very day or is very mature, cook it about five minutes in boiling water before using in this and other fresh-corn recipes.

Chapter Five

SUMMER'S END (SEPTEMBER TO OCTOBER)

The end of summer and the return of cooler weather bring a kind of second spring to farmer's fields and to CSA boxes and farmers' markets. The **young lettuce, arugula, parsley,** and **green beans** that had disappeared for a while with the heat now make one last appearance. It's time for a few last celebratory **salads** from Chapter Two.

September also brings the first of the hardier winter storage vegetables, like **winter squash** and **cabbage,** which occasionally even overlap with the last of summer's stars, fresh ripe **tomatoes.** This rare confluence is the perfect time to make **Squash-Tomato Soup** (p. 137; although, of course, this soup is also great made with canned tomatoes later in the season). While you may be cooking a lot of cabbage come winter, these last warm evenings are a good time to enjoy a **raw cabbage salad or slaw,** perhaps in one of the dressings from Chapter Two.

One thing you won't find any other time of year is **fresh shell beans.** Grab them if you see them and enjoy them right away. They cook quickly (just boil gently about 25 minutes) and are lovely with **tomatoes and lemon, dressed with a vinaigrette,** or **mashed lightly** with salt, pepper, and Parmesan.

This is also the time of year to preserve the last of summer's fresh vegetables. You can **pickle just about anything**—I have, so you can, too—and keep it in the fridge or in processed canning jars for a fresh jolt of summer later in the year.

Summer's End MENUS

Combinations that highlight the season's best

What's in Season

Arugula	Chard	Peppers
Basil	Cilantro	Potatoes
Beets	Cucumbers	Salad mix
Bitter melon	Dill	Shallots
Broccoli	Garlic	Shell beans
Cabbage	Green beans	Tomatoes
Cantaloupe	Kale	Watermelon
Carrots	Leeks	Winter squash
Cauliflower	Onions	Zucchini
	Parsley	

Slow-Roasted Tomatoes and Tomatillos

While sun-dried tomatoes traditionally get their concentrated flavor from long days under the hot, dry Mediterranean sun, we can approximate this technique in our own ovens. You do have to keep an eye on the fruit, though, because the roasting time varies tremendously by the tomatoes' size and water content.

firm-fleshed tomatoes and tomatillos

about 1 tablespoon olive oil per pound of vegetables

Heat oven to 250 degrees. Slice tomatoes in half. Remove paper covering from tomatillos, rinse tomatillos under warm water, and slice in half. Place tomatoes and tomatillos cut-side up on a baking sheet and drizzle lightly with olive oil. Roast slowly, checking on vegetables after 4 hours and every 30 to 60 minutes after that. Tomatillos roast faster than tomatoes, and smaller fruit roast faster than larger ones. Remove individual pieces when they have collapsed and shriveled but are not yet brown and hard. Store, refrigerated, in a covered glass container and submerged in oil. Use in sandwiches, salads, and stews.

Roasted Tomato and Tomatillo Puree

Place roasted tomatoes and tomatillos (see above) in bowl of food processor and, with blade running, very slowly pour oil through feed chute until it reaches a spreadable consistency. Add salt to taste. Spread on crackers or use as a sandwich spread.

Tomatillo Salsa

Tomatillos are a little more bitter than tomatoes and quite a bit firmer and less watery. I wanted a salsa that had a little zip—that's from the lime juice and the banana pepper—and also a little sweetness, for dipping and spooning onto tacos. I decided that a pinch of sugar would be a little too forward, so I added red onion and—very untraditional—a little cooling cucumber. Before using tomatillos, remove the paper covering and rub gently under warm water to remove their sticky coating.

½ red onion, coarsely chopped

½ medium cucumber, coarsely chopped

6 medium tomatillos (about 12 ounces), coarsely chopped

½ teaspoon kosher salt

½ teaspoon freshly ground black pepper

2 tablespoons olive oil

2 tablespoons lime juice

1 medium banana pepper, seeds and ribs removed, coarsely chopped

½ cup lightly chopped cilantro, leaves and stems

Place all ingredients in blender or food processor and pulse gently. Be careful not to liquefy. Taste and adjust flavors as desired. Makes about 3 cups.

Peeling Tomatoes

Most of the time, I don't bother to peel tomatoes. I find the peels add a nice texture in gazpacho and tomato sauce. But I like my **Squash-Tomato Soup** (p. 137) to be silky smooth.

To peel tomatoes, bring a big pot of water to a rolling boil. Using a sharp knife, slash a very shallow X on the bottom of each tomato. Place in boiling water a few at a time (so the temperature doesn't drop too much) and boil 1 minute, or until you see the skin start to split or pull away from the spot where you cut an X. Remove from water with a large slotted spoon or pasta server and allow to cool. When you can touch the tomatoes without burning yourself, pull off and discard the skin. Cut out the cone-shaped core at the top of the tomato and cook or chop as directed.

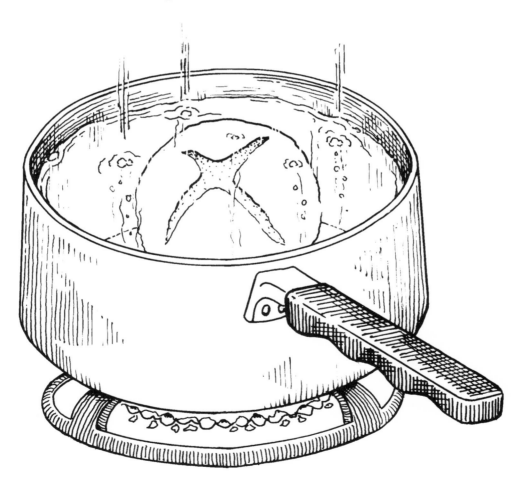

Hot Pepper–Apple Jelly

I used to make this jelly with the peels and cores left over from apple-sauce (who would want to waste all that flavor, not to mention the natural pectin?). Now I crave this jelly so much that I make applesauce with the "leftover" apples (p. 128).

Hot pepper jelly and cream cheese is a classic combination, often spread on rye crackers. It's also surprisingly good alongside a roast pork tenderloin. But my absolute favorite thing to do with it is to add it to a grilled cheese sandwich. Nothing is better with sharp Cheddar than a melty layer of hot pepper jelly, just starting to soak into the bread.

I make this recipe with jalapeños, discarding the stems and seeds, which yields a mild jelly; let's call it warm, instead of hot. You can boost the heat with serranos or cayennes or really blow the doors off with habaneros. But be sure to choose red peppers: green ones will muddy the jelly's lovely color.

> **peels and cores of 10 apples**
>
> **6 medium hot red peppers, halved, seeded if desired**
>
> **½ cup white vinegar**
>
> **4 cups sugar**

Place apple peels and cores in a large saucepan and add about 8 cups of water. Cover and boil about an hour. Strain, reserving liquid and discarding apple bits. You should have about 4 cups of liquid, depending on how tightly your lid fits and how much boiled away. If you have a little less than 4 cups, add some water. If you have a little more, no big deal, use it all.

Puree peppers with vinegar in a blender. Place liquid from apples, pepper-vinegar puree, and sugar in a wide saucepan. The mixture should not fill the pan more than halfway, as it will foam quite high as it cooks. Bring to a boil and cook, uncovered, until it passes the boiling point (212 degrees) and reaches the gelling point (220 degrees). I find a digital probe thermometer to be crucial for this step; a candy thermometer works as well, but keep a close eye on it.

Pour hot liquid through a strainer to catch and discard any stray seeds or bits of pepper. Store, refrigerated, in glass jars up to 1 month or process 10 minutes in a boiling water canner.

Variation: Don't like heat contaminating your sweets? Leave out the hot peppers and vinegar, and you've got a lovely apple jelly.

Homemade Applesauce

SERVES 4

Fresh, warm applesauce is a real treat, and it cooks up so quickly that it's easy to serve on top of homemade waffles and pancakes, which we love to have for dinner. And this sauce is a must on Grandma Lusia's Latkes (p. 178).

10 apples, peeled and cored and thinly sliced

¼ cup sugar, optional

1 tablespoon cinnamon

¼ teaspoon ground cloves

¼ teaspoon freshly grated nutmeg

pinch cayenne pepper

Stir together apple slices, sugar if using, and spices. Put a small splash of water—about a quarter cup—in a large, heavy-bottomed saucepan or Dutch oven (to keep apples from sticking). Add apple and sugar mixture. Cook over medium heat, stirring often, until apples are quite soft, about 20 minutes. For smooth applesauce, carefully puree in batches in a standing blender. For chunkier applesauce, use a stick blender right in the pan. If you like the consistency, your applesauce is done. If you'd like it a little thicker, return it to the pan, bring to a low simmer, and cook, uncovered, stirring frequently, until it's as thick as you like. A pot of boiling applesauce is like a tiny active volcano on your stove, so cover with a splatter guard as it cooks and keep tender arms away.

Variation: Use 2 tablespoons curry powder in place of the other spices.

Skordalia

Skordalia is a classic Greek dip, sometimes made with nuts or bread. I like it with potatoes as the base: they provide a completely neutral background for the garlic, which comes through so strongly you might swear it is a pureed garlic dip. I also like it because of the alchemy I watch happening in the blender. As you pour in the oil, the grainy potato mass becomes smooth and velvety.

As a dip, skordalia is better with vegetables than chips. Endive, raw zucchini, and raw green beans are great choices. You might also spread it on hearty crackers as an appetizer. Or serve it as a sauce on grilled vegetables or meat. I like to pair it with strong flavors that won't be completely overwhelmed by the garlic, especially Onion-Lemon Marinated Chicken Skewers (p. 111) or a grass-fed flank steak.

If you have any left over, you can certainly put it in the fridge, but what you'll have the next day is super-garlicky mashed potatoes, not a dip.

2 large potatoes (1 pound), peeled

5 cloves garlic, unpeeled

½ teaspoon kosher salt

2 tablespoons lemon juice

½ cup olive oil

Place potatoes and garlic in a saucepan and cover with cold water. Bring to a boil and cook until a knife slides through a potato easily, about 20 minutes; drain. Mash potatoes roughly with a fork. Squeeze garlic out of peel. Place potatoes and garlic in a blender with salt and lemon juice. With blade running, add olive oil in a thin stream. Serve warm or at room temperature, drizzled with good olive oil, the same day. Makes 3–4 cups.

Caramelized Onions

With caramelized onions in your refrigerator or freezer, you can be ready to class up just about anything, whether it's appetizers for guests or a quick sandwich for yourself. They're easy to make in huge batches and they keep very well, so I have them on hand nearly all the time.

> **5 medium onions (about 3 pounds), peeled, halved, cut into paper-thin slices**
>
> **5 large cloves garlic, peeled and cut into paper-thin slices**
>
> **1 teaspoon kosher salt**
>
> **1 tablespoon canola oil**
>
> **1 tablespoon balsamic vinegar**
>
> **1 teaspoon dried thyme or 1 large sprig fresh**

Place all ingredients in a large, heavy-bottomed pot (a Dutch oven works well). Cook, uncovered, over medium heat, stirring frequently. Keep a close eye on things and turn heat to medium low or low if onions start to brown prematurely or if you smell burning garlic. The onions should wilt and reduce well before they start to brown.

As a brown crust starts to form on the bottom of the pan, deglaze with a few extra drops of vinegar, scraping with a rubber spatula. Golden brown can turn into burnt quickly, but you want to develop as much flavor as you can. The onions should practically melt, which takes about 35 to 40 minutes. Makes 3 cups.

Seven Uses for Caramelized Onions

Straight out of the refrigerator, caramelized onions are cold, slimy, and unappealing. So warm them gently and then
- Make Caramelized Onion and Potato Tart (p. 144)
- Stir into just-cooked pasta with a little olive oil
- Spread on bruschetta
- Make an onion and tart apple sandwich

- Sprinkle with balsamic vinegar and serve next to grilled steak
- Stir into a stew or add to pot roast during cooking to deepen the flavor
- Add broth and heat for an instant onion soup

Quick-Pickled Anything

Pickling not only adds flavor; it also extends the life of any precious vegetables when your fridge threatens to overflow. While canning pickles requires some extra equipment, time, and precision, making quick pickles is as easy as pouring a hot spice and vinegar mixture over your vegetables.

A partial list of items that have ended up in jars of brine in my fridge includes cucumbers, carrots, zucchini, summer squash, cauliflower, hot peppers, corn, broccoli, green tomatoes, tomatillos, fennel, onions, and garlic. I'm sure there's been more over the years. In fact, if it's come in our CSA box, I've probably tried to pickle it.

A note on the spice mixture: I consider the dill and mustard to be de rigeur. *The rest is just based on my personal preferences. You could come up with your own mixture—just be sure to use whole spices, not ground—or buy a jar of pickling spice at the grocery store. The ingredients differ by brand, but they almost always have dill and mustard in them as well.*

Be sure to use a non-iodized salt such as kosher or pickling salt, as the iodine can make your pickled vegetables dark and cloudy.

Preparing the vegetables:

Choose vegetables with no bruises or soft spots or anything else suspect about them. Scrub thoroughly.

Cucumbers, carrots, zucchini, and summer squash: Slice on the diagonal into ⅛-inch slices.

Cauliflower and broccoli: Break into roughly bite-size florets. Peel and slice broccoli stems.

Hot peppers, small red tomatoes, and small tomatillos: Leave whole.

Onions, green tomatoes, and larger tomatillos: Cut into wedges.

Fennel: Remove fronds for another use; cut out core of bulb and slice diagonally.

Corn: Slice whole kernels off cob (see p. 101); do not milk corn cob.

Pack vegetables firmly (but without squashing them) into glass containers with lids. I find that quart jars are ideal.

For every quart of vegetables, you'll need

1 cup white vinegar

1 cup water

1 teaspoon whole mustard seeds

2 teaspoons dill seed

½ teaspoon fennel seed

2 teaspoons kosher salt

1 teaspoon whole celery seed

1 clove garlic per jar

1 hot pepper per jar

Place all ingredients in a medium saucepan. Bring to a simmer and cook 5 minutes, covered. Pour hot brine over vegetables, using a spoon to distribute spices, garlic, and hot peppers. Be sure that all vegetables are submerged and the jars are full. Store refrigerated, and wait about 5 days before using. Pickled vegetables will keep for several weeks. Discard if brine turns cloudy, vegetables discolor, or any unpleasant odor develops.

Garlic Hues

Did your pickled garlic turn blue? Don't worry! It's still edible. Two things may be to blame: garlic contains enzymes that turn blue in the presence of an acid, and it also contains sulfur compounds that can react with small amounts of copper in tap water.

Homemade Mayonnaise

Julia Child was the genius who figured out that homemade mayonnaise doesn't have to involve endless whisking while simultaneously dribbling oil drop by tiny drop—a feat which seems to require a third hand. Her simple solution? The blender. This is a simplified version of her famous recipe that I use when serving the aïoli on p. 139. Remember that the egg in this recipe is not cooked, so you must be absolutely sure you got it from a trusted source. Also be sure to use a neutral-flavored oil like canola or sunflower. I love good olive oil as much or more as the next person, but the flavor is so strong that it makes the mayonnaise inedible.

> **1 whole egg**
>
> **¼ teaspoon dry mustard**
>
> **¼ teaspoon salt**
>
> **1 tablespoon lemon juice**
>
> **½–1 cup neutral-flavored oil, such as canola or sunflower**

Place first 4 ingredients (egg through lemon juice) in a blender and blend on high for 30 seconds. Pour the oil into a small pitcher with a spout—one that will allow you to pour it excruciatingly slowly without making a mess. With the blender running and the lid on, pour the oil drop by drop through the feed hole. After about a half cup of oil, the mayonnaise should look white and thick. Keep pouring, and keep your eye on it: when oil starts pooling on top of the mayonnaise instead of being incorporated immediately, you're done! Makes about 1 cup.

Melted Leeks

SERVES 4

Who knew that the tough, stringy leek could be coaxed into a silky, decadent side dish? You could reduce the olive oil in this dish by about half; the leeks will still melt, and it will lose only a little of its richness. Don't, however, skimp on the quality of the vinegar to top it off. If all you have in the cupboard is white or cider vinegar, skip it and use lemon juice instead.

4 leeks (about 8 ounces)

¼ cup olive oil

½ teaspoon salt

1 tablespoon good balsamic vinegar or lemon juice

Trim roots, but leave enough of the base of the leek that it holds together. Slit each leek lengthwise into quarters, starting about half an inch from the root end. Trim off the really tough green parts, but not too much. Rinse leeks well to remove sand and grit.

Place leeks in a wide-bottomed saucepan large enough to hold them in a single layer. Add water to about halfway up the leeks. Add olive oil and salt. Cover and bring to a rolling boil. Cover loosely and boil 30 minutes, keeping an eye on the water level: you want most of the water to boil off, but you don't want the pan to dry out and burn.

Heat oven to 325 degrees. Transfer leeks and any remaining liquid to an oven-safe baking dish and bake 40 minutes, until golden brown. Top with vinegar or lemon juice to serve.

Melted Leeks with Eggs

For a lovely supper, after the leeks have baked, crack 1 egg per person on top (no shame if it's just you alone) and cover and bake an additional 5 to 10 minutes, depending on how you like your eggs.

Spicy Deep-Fried Cauliflower

SERVES 6–8

Deep-frying your vegetables does seem like a cop out. But these party treats are light and crispy—not coated in batter—and, most important, still have the sweet, crunchy cauliflower flavor.

> **1 cup flour**
>
> **2 teaspoons kosher salt**
>
> **1 teaspoon freshly ground black pepper**
>
> **½ teaspoon cayenne pepper**
>
> **2 teaspoons ground cumin**
>
> **2 teaspoons ground coriander**
>
> **1 head cauliflower, cut into 1-inch florets**
>
> **oil**

Stir together flour, salt, pepper, and spices. Toss with cauliflower florets. In a heavy-bottomed saucepan, heat 3 inches of oil to 375 degrees. Use a candy or probe thermometer to monitor the temperature: if it cools off too much, you get greasy and soggy instead of crispy and light. Heat oven to 200 degrees.

Take a handful of cauliflower florets and shake off the extra flour, being sure that they are thoroughly coated. Drop individually into hot oil and cook 3 to 4 minutes, until very lightly browned. Remove florets to a baking sheet and place in oven. Repeat with remaining florets. Serve hot.

Beet Greens

SERVES 4

*Spinach lovers who have not yet discovered beet greens, take note:
oft-neglected beet tops are a meatier, muskier, tangier version of that more
popular green, without as much of the weird tannic note that makes the back
of your teeth feel gritty. I love them. In fact, this is often my cook's treat while
I roast the beetroots themselves.*

*Because beets are usually sold for their roots and not their leaves, you may
need to take extra care to sort through the leaves, discarding any that are
sunburned or bruised.*

> **1 tablespoon olive oil**
>
> **1 bunch beet greens, rinsed, stems removed**
>
> **salt and freshly ground black pepper to taste**
>
> **¼ cup water**
>
> **balsamic vinegar to taste**

Heat oil in a wide sauté pan with lid over medium-high heat. Add greens,
stir to coat, and cook until wilted, about 2 minutes. Stir salt and pepper into water, pour over greens, and cover immediately. Cook about 5
minutes, until tender. Serve with balsamic vinegar.

SOUPS

Squash-Tomato Soup

SERVES 6

Most recipes for squash soup are based on apple cider or just squash and cream. But squash is entirely lacking in acidity. Tomatoes, it turns out, have that complex tartness squash needs. The key here is that you've got at least equal parts tomato and squash (I sometimes up the ratio of tomatoes even more). If you're using whole tomatoes, peel them first (see p. 126). For more on roasting and pureeing squash, see p. 138.

> 1 large shallot, finely chopped
>
> ½ large onion, finely chopped (about 1 cup)
>
> 2 large cloves garlic, finely chopped
>
> 1 dried red pepper, sliced
>
> 2 teaspoons dried oregano
>
> 1 teaspoon salt
>
> 2 tablespoons oil
>
> 4 cups winter squash puree
>
> 4 cups crushed tomatoes in their own juice
>
> 1 cup heavy cream
>
> 1 tablespoon balsamic vinegar, or to taste
>
> crumbled blue cheese, optional

Place first 7 ingredients (shallot through oil) in a large, heavy-bottomed saucepan set over medium-low heat. Stirring occasionally, cook until onions are soft and translucent. Add squash and tomatoes and bring to a simmer.

Use a stick blender to puree and fully mix all ingredients, or blend in batches in a standing blender and then return the soup to the pan. (If you use a standing blender, fill the pitcher no more than halfway and then place a dish towel over the lid and hold it down firmly with your hand. Hot liquids in a blender can explode.) Add cream and gently heat through. Serve with balsamic vinegar and/or blue cheese.

Winter Squash Puree

You can use just about any kind of winter squash to make your puree, although some, like hubbards, tend to be a little more watery. I do try to save delicatas for pan roasting (see p. 178) and butternuts for chili (p. 177), but they make lovely purees, as well.

To make squash puree, cut squash in half vertically, scoop out and discard seeds (or roast them: see below), place cut-side down on a rimmed baking sheet, and bake at 400 degrees until pressing a finger against the skin leaves an impression. The timing will vary greatly by the size and type of squash, so start checking after about 20 minutes but allow up to 40 for large, hard squashes. Cool slightly and then scoop out flesh and puree in a food processor. Use in Squash-Tomato Soup (p. 137), Squash Lasagna (p. 175), Pumpkin Bread (p. 185), Pumpkin Bread Pancakes (p. 184), or Polenta with Squash (p. 175) or freeze in one- or two-cup batches for future use.

Roasted Squash Seeds

Scoop seeds into a bowl of water and allow to sit for 30 minutes to an hour, to loosen pulp. Rub between your hands to help release the seeds. Heat oven to 375 degrees. Spread seeds on a towel to dry slightly and then transfer to a rimmed baking sheet. Sprinkle with coarse salt and paprika, using fingertips to distribute salt well. Bake 10 to 15 minutes, stirring often and listening for "pops" that tell you your seeds are exploding.

Most squash seeds roast well, but I've found that larger seeds (seeds from a turban squash are about the size of a lima bean) are too tough to enjoy and tend to explode in the oven, anyway.

MOSTLY MAIN DISHES

Le Grand Aïoli

SERVES 4–8

A big, festive platter of poached fish and boiled vegetables is a traditional summer dish in Provence, where aïoli *refers to both the garlicky mayonnaise and the feast that celebrates it. The mix of vegetables isn't important, but their presentation is: heap the platter high and let everyone pick what appeals to them—a little fish, a little potato, a little beet, a lot of mayonnaise. Cooked chickpeas seasoned with salt, pepper, and herbs can be substituted for the fish.*

> **2 large cloves garlic, grated or pressed through a garlic press**
>
> **double batch mayonnaise (p. 133)**
>
> **2–3 pounds vegetables: beets, broccoli, carrots, cauliflower, green beans, potatoes, tomatoes**
>
> **2 cups vegetable, fish, or chicken broth**
>
> **salt and freshly ground black pepper to taste**
>
> **1–2 pounds mild white fish, such as haddock or cod (about 4–6 ounces per person)**
>
> **8 hard-cooked eggs, cut into wedges**
>
> **lemon wedges**

Stir garlic into mayonnaise and set aside. Prepare the vegetables: peel beets and carrots and cut into large, attractive pieces; separate broccoli and cauliflower into florets; top and tail green beans; cut potatoes and tomatoes into wedges. Everything but the tomatoes will be boiled until just tender.

Bring a large pot of generously salted water to a boil and set a bowl of ice water or a large colander in the sink. Beets need to boil for at least 30 minutes, until tender, and need their own water so they don't turn everything pink. Everything else can be boiled in succession and scooped out into the ice water or colander and rinsed with cold water. Boil potatoes 15 minutes, carrots 8 minutes, cauliflower and broccoli 5 minutes, green beans 3 minutes.

In a wide sauté pan with a lid, bring the broth to a boil. Season fish fillets and place in pan. Cover immediately, turn off heat, and allow to poach 10 to 15 minutes, until flaky.

On a big, beautiful platter, arrange fish, vegetables, eggs, lemon wedges, and bowls of garlicky mayonnaise.

Palak Paneer

SERVES 4

I wish this were a recipe I learned at the elbow of a dear Indian friend, but it's not. It's my own version, and I take full responsibility for any deviations from tradition. I created it to satisfy a strong and rather frequent craving for this rich and creamy Indian treat. The big difference is that my version is rich in flavor without too much oil or any cream. Cooking the spices with the onions intensifies the flavor, and the long simmer melds it all together. Serve with rice and a simple salad of sliced onions and tomatoes.

You can find paneer—a fresh Indian cheese—in most grocery stores, but it's very easy to make your own. Cubed firm tofu also makes a fine substitute.

1 medium onion, halved and thinly sliced

6 cloves garlic, peeled

2 tablespoons olive oil or ghee (clarified butter)

½ teaspoon kosher salt

2 teaspoons ground cumin

2 teaspoons ground coriander

½ teaspoon asafetida (see p. 104)

¼ teaspoon turmeric

- **1 dried red pepper, seeded if desired, thinly sliced, optional**
- **1 (1-inch) piece fresh ginger, peeled and grated**
- **1 medium tomato, cored and roughly chopped**
- **10 ounces fresh spinach**
- **½ cup water**
- **freshly grated nutmeg**
- **1 batch Paneer (recipe follows) or 8 ounces firm tofu, cubed**

Place onions, garlic, oil or ghee, and spices (salt through ginger) in a large sauté pan with a lid over medium-low heat. Cook, stirring occasionally, until very soft and fragrant but not brown, about 20 minutes. If the mixture starts to stick, add a tablespoon of water at a time and scrape the bottom of the pan. Add tomato, spinach, and water. The volume of the spinach will greatly reduce, so just pack it on top of the mixture. Cover and cook on low for 1 hour, stirring occasionally.

Use a stick blender to blend everything very well in the pan, being sure to break up large pieces. (If you use a standing blender instead, be very careful: work in batches, filling the pitcher no more than halfway, and use a kitchen towel and a firm hand to hold the lid on.) Grate a little fresh nutmeg into the spinach mixture and gently add the paneer or tofu cubes.

Paneer

Of course you can buy paneer, but it's almost easier to make it with what you have in your kitchen than it is to put on your shoes and run to the store. Any kind of milk will work, but I strongly recommend whole, or even two percent, over skim, which will make a rubbery and unsatisfying cheese.

- **½ gallon milk**
- **¼ cup lemon juice or white vinegar**

In a heavy-bottomed saucepan, bring milk to a simmer. Watch vigilantly for bubbles around the edges, and don't let the milk come to a full boil. When bubbles appear, turn off the heat, quickly stir in the lemon juice or vinegar, cover, and let sit for 10 minutes. You should have whitish curd floating in yellowish-greenish whey.

Line a colander with cheesecloth and strain the curd. When most of the liquid has drained off, lift up the cheesecloth, wrap it in a flat-ish bundle, and place it on a plate. Place another plate on top with something to weight it down, like a heavy can. Let sit for half an hour to release the rest of the liquid. Unwrap cheesecloth and slice paneer into roughly 1-inch cubes.

Vegetable Tarts

These tarts are elegant and easy. As appetizers, they really need to pack a punch, so choose strongly flavored cheeses. I've made all of these in the past using a pâte brisée (a short pastry) for the crust, but I wanted something simpler, so I pulled some puff pastry out of the freezer. There's no shame in using frozen puff pastry: while DIY is a laudable goal, there are some things the pros do much better than most of us ever could in our home kitchens. Be sure to cook the tarts thoroughly: you don't want the middle pieces to have droopy pastry.

For each tart, thaw 1 sheet of puff pastry according to package directions and place on a lightly greased pan. Heat oven to 400 degrees. Top as instructed and bake 35 to 40 minutes, until edges are puffed and golden brown. Slice into 2-inch squares and serve. The beet tart needs to cool completely before slicing, but the others can be served warm.

➤ Beet and Goat Cheese Tart

SERVES 8 AS AN APPETIZER

Think of your classic beet salad: slice beets, drizzle with balsamic vinegar, and sprinkle with goat cheese. It's good. Now think about baking that in a buttery, salty crust, and you've got a perfect appetizer. Dried sumac is a common Middle Eastern spice that adds a little tartness and makes this dish lovely to look at, but if you don't have it, don't let that hold you back. The honey may be an unexpected twist, but it amplifies the earthy sweetness of the beets and makes this tart almost worthy of dessert.

> 1 pound beets
>
> ½ cup plain nonfat yogurt
>
> 1 egg
>
> 6 ounces goat cheese
>
> 1 sheet frozen puff pastry, thawed
>
> olive oil
>
> 1–2 tablespoons honey, optional
>
> 1 teaspoon dried sumac (see head note)

Wrap beets in aluminum foil and roast in a 400-degree oven until a knife slides easily all the way through. How long this step takes varies greatly with the size of the beets, but count on about an hour. For this recipe, I cook my beets a little longer than I might for other uses, so they are quite soft. Leave oven on. Peel beets under running water as soon as they are cool enough to touch, and then slice about ¼ inch thick.

Mix together yogurt, egg, and goat cheese. Place pastry on lightly floured or parchment-lined baking sheet. Brush very lightly with olive oil. Cover pastry with overlapping disks of beets, leaving about 1 inch around the edges. Spoon goat cheese mixture over the top, still leaving the edges clear. Drizzle with honey if desired, and sprinkle with sumac. Bake as directed on p. 142.

✒ Caramelized Onion and Potato Tart

SERVES 8 AS AN APPETIZER

> 1 sheet frozen puff pastry, thawed
>
> 1 medium potato, scrubbed, sliced paper thin
>
> 1 cup Caramelized Onions (p. 130)
>
> ½ cup Idiazabal or other strongly flavored medium-hard cheese, finely grated (2 ounces)

Layer potatoes on pastry sheet, overlapping slightly, leaving ½-inch border. Spread onions over potatoes. Sprinkle cheese on top, covering border, too. Bake as directed on p. 142.

✒ Chard and Blue Cheese Tart

SERVES 8 AS AN APPETIZER

> 2 small bunches rainbow chard
>
> 1 tablespoon olive oil
>
> ½ teaspoon fresh rosemary, lightly crushed
>
> 1 sheet frozen puff pastry, thawed
>
> 3 ounces blue cheese, crumbled

Remove leaves from rainbow chard and reserve for another use. Slice stems into 1-inch pieces, to yield about 2 cups. Heat olive oil in sauté pan over medium-high heat. Add chard stems and rosemary and cook until lightly browned, about 5 minutes. Add about 2 tablespoons water and cover. Steam until slightly soft, about 5 minutes. Spread chard on puff pastry, leaving ½-inch border. Sprinkle with blue cheese. Bake as directed on p. 142.

Pasta with Sautéed Vegetables

SERVES 4

This is among the quickest and easiest summer dinners I can imagine. The vegetables cook while the pasta boils, and dinner is on the table in less than twenty minutes. I use whole wheat pasta: it's heartier, more flavorful, and more filling. While I normally sauté almost everything in olive oil, I like the richness butter adds to this simple and very healthful dish. Adding salt after cooking, rather than while sautéing, keeps the vegetables from releasing too much water.

If you're not drowning in zucchini and tomatoes, eggplant and green peppers make a nice variation. Cut both into half-inch pieces. Cook eggplant first, about five minutes. Add peppers and cook five minutes more. Don't be afraid to go heavy on the vegetables. The pasta is very much in a supporting role here.

½ **pound whole wheat penne**

2 **tablespoons butter**

2 **small or 1 medium zucchini or summer squash, cut into matchsticks (1 to 2 inches long and ⅛-inch thick)**

2 **medium tomatoes, chopped into ½-inch pieces (about 2 cups)**

¼ **cup basil chiffonade (at left) or roughly chopped cilantro**

2 **tablespoons balsamic or other flavorful vinegar**

salt and pepper

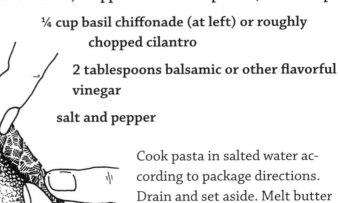

Cook pasta in salted water according to package directions. Drain and set aside. Melt butter in a large sauté pan over medium-high heat. When bubbling subsides, add zucchini and cook, stirring, about 3 minutes. Add tomatoes and basil or cilantro and cook, stirring, another 3 minutes. Stir in cooked pasta and heat through, about 1 minute. Remove from heat and stir in vinegar and salt and pepper to taste. This dish is delicious hot and at room temperature

Vegetarian Stuffed Peppers

SERVES 4

I was never really a fan of stuffed peppers. I associated them with dried out, overcooked peppers and bland meat stuffing. And they were so hard to eat! My husband, however, loves them. I finally relented and came up with a version that we both enjoy. I solve the hard-to-eat problem by cutting the peppers in half through the top (vertically), into wide, shallow boats, rather than cutting off the tops and stuffing them standing up. The peppers don't get dried out because they're nestled in chopped tomatoes and steam while they cook. And I replace the traditional meat stuffing with nutty, chewy, flavorful farro—a protein-packed variety of wheat also known as emmer wheat.

1 tablespoon plus 1 teaspoon coarse salt

⅔ cup semi-pearled farro

2 tablespoons oil

1 medium onion, chopped (about 1 cup)

1 tablespoon chopped garlic (about 1 large clove)

1 teaspoon caraway seeds

4 medium green bell peppers

8 ounces mushrooms (crimini are a good choice), wiped clean and finely chopped

plenty of freshly ground black pepper

1 teaspoon paprika

¼ cup chopped parsley

1 (15-ounce) can diced tomatoes, or 2 cups fresh tomatoes, peeled and chopped

1–2 teaspoons pimenton de la vera (smoked Spanish paprika)

Heat oven to 375 degrees. Bring a medium pot of water to a boil and add 1 tablespoon of the salt. Add farro and boil, uncovered, 20 minutes. Farro should retain a little springy crunch. Drain and set aside.

Place oil, onions, garlic, caraway seeds, and remaining 1 teaspoon salt in a large sauté pan over medium heat and cook until soft. Chop 1 of the peppers into ¼-inch pieces, add to onions, and cook a minute or two, until soft. Add mushrooms to pan, increasing heat to medium high. Cook until liquid given off by mushrooms evaporates, so the mixture is relatively dry. Remove from heat and stir in black pepper, paprika, and parsley.

Mix about two-thirds of the mushroom mixture with the farro to make a stuffing. Stir tomatoes into remaining mushroom mixture and heat through to make a sauce.

Cut out stems of remaining peppers. Slice in half lengthwise and dig out ribs and cores with fingers. Spread tomato mixture in pan large enough to hold all pepper halves, cut-side up. Spoon stuffing into peppers and arrange on top of tomato mixture. Cover with aluminum foil and bake 40 minutes. Sprinkle with pimenton de la vera before serving.

Fresh Shell Beans with Basil and Lemon

SERVES 4

If you see fresh shell beans at the market or if they come in your CSA share, cancel your plans for the evening: you're staying home and making these beans. Fresh shell beans—they come in many varieties, but just about any will shine when prepared this way—are the same beans that get dried and bagged, but fresh off they vine they are firm and creamy and full of flavor. Once they're picked, though, you've got about twenty-four to forty-eight hours before they lose some of their magic and start going starchy (or worse, moldy, which happens very easily). Fresh beans are almost always sold in their pods, but popping a bowlful of pods out on the front step on an early September evening is part of the pleasure.

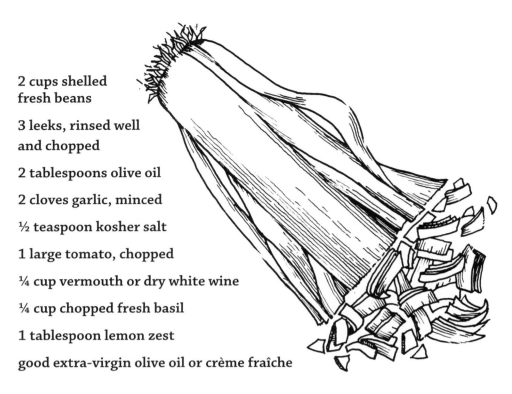

2 cups shelled
fresh beans

3 leeks, rinsed well
and chopped

2 tablespoons olive oil

2 cloves garlic, minced

½ teaspoon kosher salt

1 large tomato, chopped

¼ cup vermouth or dry white wine

¼ cup chopped fresh basil

1 tablespoon lemon zest

good extra-virgin olive oil or crème fraîche

Bring a large pot of salted water to a boil. Add beans and cook 25 minutes, until tender but not mushy. Drain.

While beans are cooking, place leeks, olive oil, garlic, and salt in a wide sauté pan. Turn heat to medium and cook slowly, stirring often, about 15 minutes. The leeks should soften completely before they start taking on a light golden brown color. Reduce the heat if they start to brown too fast; you don't want them to be crispy. Add tomato and vermouth and cook, stirring often, 10 minutes, until tomatoes and leeks meld together. Add drained beans, basil, and lemon zest and cook about 2 minutes. Serve warm or at room temperature, with a drizzle of very good olive oil or a dollop of crème fraîche.

Bitter Melon and Chicken Stir-Fry

SERVES 4

There is nothing in the plant kingdom that quite lives up to its name like bitter melon. One way to tone down that bitterness a bit is to parboil it, which I strongly suggest for the uninitiated. The sauce in this stir-fry—which is in no way authentically Hmong—plays hot, sour, and sweet flavors against the melon's intense bitterness to become very potent and satisfying.

3 tablespoons rice vinegar

½–1 teaspoon sriracha chili sauce

1 teaspoon sugar

3 tablespoons soy sauce

3 tablespoons sake or chicken broth

1 teaspoon cornstarch

¼–½ teaspoon red pepper flakes

2 bitter melons, halved, seeds and pith removed, cut into ½-inch-thick slices (about 2 cups)

1 tablespoon sesame oil

4 boneless, skinless chicken thighs (about 8–10 ounces), thinly sliced

1 large clove garlic, minced

Stir together rice vinegar, sriracha, sugar, soy sauce, sake or chicken broth, cornstarch, and red pepper flakes and set aside. Bring a medium pot of salted water to a boil. Add bitter melon and boil 3 minutes; drain and set aside.

Heat sesame oil in a large sauté pan over medium-high heat. Add chicken and cook, stirring, until thoroughly cooked and very crispy and brown. Remove to a plate. Add bitter melon to pan and cook, stirring, about 2 minutes, until beginning to brown. Add garlic and cook, stirring, until fragrant, about 1 minute. Return chicken and any accumulated juices to pan. Turn off heat and quickly add sauce mixture, stirring until thickened. Serve immediately.

Spaghetti with Roasted Tomato Sauce

SERVES 4

Roasting brings out a warmer, sweeter flavor in tomatoes than cooking them on the stove top does. In the blender, this sauce will turn a pale, creamy color as the oil and tomato mixture emulsifies.

> 2 pounds tomatoes
>
> 1 large onion, sliced into wedges
>
> ¼ cup olive oil
>
> 6 cloves garlic, unpeeled
>
> ½ teaspoon kosher salt
>
> 1 pound spaghetti

Heat oven to 350 degrees. Core tomatoes and slice in half vertically. Remove seeds and all the goopy stuff around them (a grapefruit spoon is perfect for this task), working over a mesh strainer set in a cup to reserve the juices for another recipe (see p. 151). Discard seeds and pulp.

Arrange tomatoes and onion on a rimmed baking sheet and drizzle with olive oil. Gently rub the oil into the vegetables with your hands. Add garlic cloves to pan. Bake 1 hour, until tomatoes have started to shrivel and droop.

Fish out the garlic cloves and squeeze garlic onto tomatoes and onions. A good way to do this is to grip each one in a kitchen towel and snip the end off with scissors. Tip the entire contents of the tray, juices and all, into a blender (you could use a food processor, but some brands will leak if you put this much liquid in), add salt, and pulse gently.

Put a large pot of water on to boil and cook spaghetti according to package directions. Drain pasta and toss with 2 cups of sauce. Freeze the other half for up to 3 months.

Cook's Treat

When you seed the tomatoes, be sure to catch all the juices and strain out the seeds and pulp. The juice you catch is delicious, especially if you put it in the blender with a handful of ice, some salt and pepper, paprika, and hot sauce.

SWEETS AND TREATS

Zucchini-Lime Bar Cookies

MAKES 12 BARS

Moist and mild zucchini is a natural in baked goods. Rolled oats make these bar cookies chewy and more substantial than a quick bread. If you use quick-cooking oats, expect the cookies to be softer. You can also add a little more whole-grain flavor by substituting whole wheat flour for half the all-purpose flour. The tangy lime flavor is a nice change from zucchini's usual friends, cinnamon and cloves.

½ cup butter (1 stick), at room temperature

½ cup packed brown sugar

½ cup sugar

1 egg

2 cups grated zucchini

zest of 2 limes

1 cup all-purpose flour

½ teaspoon baking soda

½ teaspoon salt

2 cups rolled oats (see head note)

¼ cup freshly squeezed lime juice

2 cups powdered sugar

Heat oven to 350 degrees. Grease a 9x13-inch pan. Beat together butter and sugars. Beat in egg until thoroughly mixed. Stir in zucchini and lime zest.

In a separate bowl, whisk together flour, baking soda, and salt. Stir into butter mixture. Stir in oats. Dough will be thick and sticky. Spread into prepared pan. Bake 35 minutes, until firm and barely golden brown. Let cool completely.

Stir together lime juice and powdered sugar to make a thick but pourable glaze. Add a little more sugar or a little more juice to adjust the consistency if necessary. Drizzle on cooled bars and spread gently with a spatula. Allow to set. Cut into squares.

Spiced Chocolate Beet Cake

SERVES 8

This recipe is not a way to sneak vegetables into your or anyone else's diet. The beets serve an important culinary function: they keep this cake moist, almost gooey. They also make it a delicious deep, dark brown. It's a little too gooey to turn out of the pan, so leave it in and dress it up with a dusting of spiced sugar.

For the cake

1½ pounds beets, trimmed

1½ cups sugar

1 cup full-fat plain yogurt

3 eggs, at room temperature, beaten well

1 teaspoon vanilla

2 cups flour

¾ cup unsweetened cocoa powder

2 teaspoons baking soda

1 teaspoon salt

1 teaspoon ground ginger

¼ teaspoon freshly grated nutmeg

½ teaspoon ground cloves

2 teaspoons ground cinnamon

For the topping

¼ cup powdered sugar

⅛ teaspoon freshly grated nutmeg

1 tablespoon unsweetened cocoa powder

⅛ teaspoon ground cloves

¼ teaspoon ground ginger

1 teaspoon cinnamon

Heat oven to 350 degrees. Grease and flour a 9x13-inch baking pan. Place beets in a saucepan with enough water to cover. Cook 1½ hours, until a fork pierces them easily (the timing varies greatly depending on the size of your beets). Remove from water and let cool until you can handle them, and then peel under cool running water. Chop roughly and whirl in a food processor to make a puree.

Mix together 2 cups beet puree, sugar, yogurt, eggs, and vanilla. In a separate bowl, whisk together dry ingredients (flour through cinnamon). Fold dry ingredients lightly into beet mixture. Pour into prepared pan. Bake 40 minutes, until a cake tester comes out dry. Let cake cool completely in pan. Whisk together topping ingredients and sprinkle over the top using a sifter or mesh strainer.

Minty Melon Granita

SERVES 6–8

Crisp, cold, and minty, this granita is both refreshing and extraordinarily easy to pull together. Most granita recipes call for stirring and scraping every half hour or so, but the melon and sugar in this recipe mean that you can forget about it in the freezer and give it just one trip through the mixer. Honeydew is ideal for this recipe, but cantaloupe and watermelon work well, too.

½ cup sugar

1 cup water

6 cups melon, peeled, seeded, cut into 1-inch cubes

¼ cup lime juice

12 mint leaves

⅛ teaspoon kosher salt

In a small saucepan, dissolve sugar in water and simmer 1 minute. Let cool completely. Place all ingredients in a blender and pulse until very well combined. Freeze in a relatively shallow bowl 6 to 8 hours or overnight. Break up frozen block with your fingers (it should be very soft because of the sugar content) and place it in the bowl of a standing mixer fitted with the whisk attachment. Whisk well, about 1 minute, until fluffy, like shaved ice. (A food processor will also work for this step, but be especially vigilant not to overheat and melt the granita.)

Melon-Vodka Slushie

SERVES 8

If you've got an almost-overripe melon on your counter, save it from the compost pile by scooping out the seeds, removing the peel, and cutting it into small cubes. Spread the cubes on baking sheets or plates to freeze, and then store them in plastic bags. Now you're most of the way toward a delicious late-summer dessert drink. I've made this with watermelon, cantaloupe, and honeydew.

For a nonalcoholic version, substitute apple juice for the vodka. This swap adds a little sweetness, which the kids appreciate. The ratio of vodka to melon is up to you.

> **6 cups melon, peeled, seeded, cut into 1-inch cubes**
>
> **½ cup freshly squeezed lime juice**
>
> **pinch salt**
>
> **2 cups vodka**

Freeze melon in a single layer on trays overnight or until solid. Place melon cubes in bowl of blender or food processor, and add lime juice, salt, and vodka. Puree until mixture is the texture of a slushie.

Chapter Six

AUTUMN HARVEST (OCTOBER TO NOVEMBER)

Dark, cold evenings and sun-filled, chilly weekend days are perfect for big cooking projects. Roast up a big pan full of **winter squash;** make a few tubs full of **Caramelized Onions** (p. 130) to keep in the refrigerator and freezer; fill your own and your friends' fridges with **Celeriac Attack Soup** (p. 171) and **Sweet Potato Blue Cheese Soup** (p. 173). When you've got any of these things on hand, you're more than halfway to a satisfying meal.

Now is the time to reacquaint yourself with **brussels sprouts.** You may think you don't like them, probably because you haven't had them cut fresh from the stalk just hours (or maybe a day) before they were cooked. Like so many vegetables, brussels sprouts start going starchy after they're picked. You might find them in the store at other times of year, but now is when they are at their absolute best. If you're lucky, your CSA or farmers' market might have them right on the stalk.

Thanks to cold frames and such, you'll still find some green things in your CSA box and at the farmers' market. Many of these, like **broccoli, arugula, spinach,** and **peppers,** are especially delicious after a cold snap. Root vegetables like **carrots** and **parsnips** and tubers like **potatoes, sweet potatoes, celeriac,** and **sunchokes** are in full force now. Your oven may be busy every evening, **roasting** a mixture of these with some herbs. This time of year is also when many of us turn back to the roasted and braised meats that cool weather seems to call for. Next time you make a pot roast, you might try doubling or tripling the vegetables you roast with it. The roast will stretch farther and the delicious vegetables will get gobbled up.

Autumn Harvest MENUS

Combinations that highlight the season's best

What's in Season

Arugula	Cornmeal	Peppers
Beets	Dill	Potatoes
Broccoli	Dried beans	Radishes
Brussels sprouts	Garlic	Rutabagas
Cabbage	Herbs	Shallots
Carrots	Kale	Spinach
Cauliflower	Leeks	Sweet potatoes
Celeriac	Onions	Turnips
Chard	Parsley	Winter squash
Cilantro	Parsnips	

Your Ersatz Root Cellar

Around this time of year we get the last of our CSA boxes. We eat the brussels sprouts and cold frame spinach right away, and I start counting down the days until we eat the last farmer carrot, the last celeriac, the last potato, the last squash. While we'll eventually eat them up, I'd kick myself if we ever let them go to waste. Stored properly, most of those things will keep for weeks, if not months.

Generations ago, this meant storage in a root cellar. Now it means paper bags in my unheated garage. You want a cool but not freezing spot (50 degrees Fahrenheit is about right). You want your vegetables to be kept in the dark and absolutely free from excess moisture but not in airtight containers. Potatoes, sweet potatoes, turnips, celeriac, and winter squash get individual paper bags. (Winter squash will also keep several weeks right on the counter.) Parsnips, carrots, and cabbage I keep in plastic bags in the low-moisture side of my crisper.

CONDIMENTS

Pumpkin Butter

This concoction is like pumpkin bread in a jar: sweet and spicy. It makes a nice hostess gift and is tasty on toast in the morning. Although you can use any kind of winter squash puree here (see p. 138 for more on roasting and pureeing), it seems safer to call this "pumpkin butter." Pumpkin sounds cozy and fall-like; squash sounds like "You're not getting up from this table until you finish your dinner, young lady."

Do not seal pumpkin butter in canning jars! It is too low in acid to preserve this way and deadly bacteria could grow. Keep it in the fridge for up to a few weeks. It also freezes nicely, for up to 3 months.

4 cups winter squash puree

3 cups sugar

2 teaspoons ground cardamom

1 tablespoon cinnamon

2 teaspoons ground ginger

1 teaspoon ground cloves

Combine all ingredients in a heavy-bottomed saucepan set over medium heat and bring to a boil. Boiling sugar is like hot lava, so keep a splatter guard on hand. Stirring frequently (constantly, near the end) to keep a crust from forming on the bottom, boil until the mixture has turned a nice, caramelly brown. Transfer to jars or glass containers and let cool. Makes about 6 cups.

SALADS AND OTHER SIDES

Barbecue Sunchoke Chips

While only distant cousins of the artichoke (they're both members of the daisy family), sunchokes do have a little bit of the artichoke's musky, springy flavor. This detail may or may not be the origin of their other name—Jerusalem artichokes. They fry up like potatoes and taste delicious with this homemade barbecue flavor mix. Some farmers overwinter their sunchokes, so you may find a nice selection in the spring as well.

2 pounds sunchokes, peeled (see p. 160) and thinly sliced on a mandoline

1 cup white vinegar

oil

½ teaspoon kosher salt

1 teaspoon sugar

1 teaspoon pimenton de la vera (smoked Spanish paprika) or paprika

As you slice the sunchokes, transfer slices immediately to vinegar to prevent browning. Pat dry before frying. Pour about 3 inches of oil into a medium saucepan and heat to 300 degrees, using a candy thermometer or an instant-read thermometer to monitor the temperature.

Working in batches to maintain the oil's temperature, gently drop about one-third of the sunchoke slices into the oil. Cook until limp but not brown, 2 to 3 minutes. Remove to a paper towel–lined plate to drain. Repeat with remaining sunchokes.

When you have blanched all the chips, heat the oil to 375 degrees. Again, working in batches and keeping a close eye on the temperature, return sunchokes to oil and cook until brown, about 3 minutes. Meanwhile, stir together salt, sugar, and pimenton or paprika. Drain chips briefly on paper towels and toss with salt mixture while still hot.

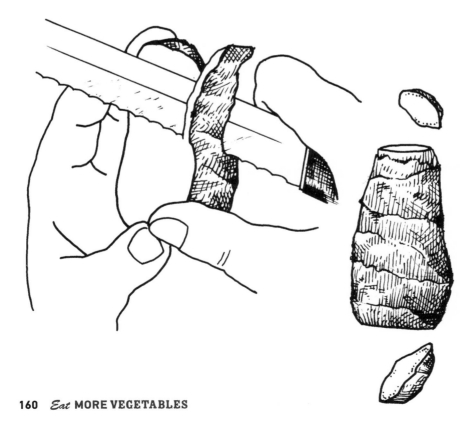

Roasted Radishes

SERVES 2–4

There's really no reason to roast the radishes you get in the early summer. You probably don't want to heat the oven and, if you're like me, those radishes disappeared before you could finish stashing everything in the fridge. But the fall crop comes at a time when you've probably got the oven going for something else anyway, and when a hot, buttery something special alongside dinner sounds very nice. When roasted, radishes lose all their peppery fire and turn almost sweet. These are almost candy-like in the joy they inspire.

> **1 bunch radishes (French breakfast radishes are best), trimmed**
>
> **1 tablespoon butter**
>
> **1 teaspoon salt**
>
> **fleur de sel or sea salt**

Heat oven to 425 degrees. Place radishes in a baking dish with butter and salt and set in the oven. Once the butter has melted, give the dish a little shake to coat the radishes. Roast about 35 minutes, until just tender but still crunchy. Serve immediately, topped with fancy salt.

Hog's Back Potatoes Gratin

SERVES 6–8

Although a simple, classic dish, potatoes gratin eluded me for a long time. I was trying to re-create my grandmother's version, with only her "enough potatoes, enough milk" recipe to guide me. When I asked Grandma how she kept hers from splitting or turning soupy, she answered, "Well, that's the trick, isn't it?" And then David Van Eeckhout offered his family's recipe in the newsletter that comes every week with the Hog's Back Farm CSA share. Perfection. With sliced ham and pie for dessert, it's just like dinner at Grandma's. (The trick, by the way, to keeping it from splitting is to watch the heat. If your oven runs hot, turn it down.)

3 tablespoons butter

2 cloves garlic, chopped

3 medium shallots, very thinly sliced

1½ cups heavy cream

½ teaspoon freshly grated nutmeg

1 sprig thyme

2 pounds starchy potatoes, peeled and cut into ⅛-inch-thick slices

kosher salt and freshly ground black pepper to taste

½ cup freshly grated Parmesan, plus 2 tablespoons for broiling (about 2½ ounces)

Heat oven to 350 degrees. In a saucepan over medium heat, melt butter and cook garlic and shallots until soft but not brown, about 5 minutes. Add cream, nutmeg, and thyme, bring to a simmer (bubbles will form around the outside of the pan, but it should not come to a rolling boil), and then remove from heat. Meanwhile, grease a 7x11-inch baking dish. Arrange one-third of the potatoes in the pan, overlapping the slices. Season with salt and pepper. Pour one-third of the cream over the top. Sprinkle with one-third of the Parmesan. Make 2 more layers, ending with the Parmesan. Bake, uncovered, 1 hour to 75 minutes, until potatoes are very soft when pierced with a knife. Your patience will be rewarded. Remove cover, sprinkle with remaining 2 tablespoons Parmesan, and broil until cheese browns, about 5 minutes.

Remoulade

SERVES 4

A classic French accompaniment to roast beef, remoulade seems festive to me, perhaps because my husband's family invariably serves it on the holiday buffet, or maybe because the combination of the rich mayonnaise and sharp horseradish is right at home during the winter holidays. Serve it as a side salad, or pile it high on a sandwich.

While I almost always choose my box grater over the food processor, this is one instance where I reach for the machine with the motor. Celeriac is very hard, and in remoulade the longer strands from the food processor aren't as unattractive as I find them in other recipes.

> 1 medium celeriac, peeled (see p. 172) and grated (see head note)
>
> 2 tablespoons freshly squeezed lemon juice
>
> 1 medium green apple, quartered, cored, and grated
>
> 1 cup mayonnaise (p. 133)
>
> ¼ cup whole-grain mustard
>
> kosher salt and freshly ground black pepper to taste
>
> 1 tablespoon prepared horseradish, optional

Toss celeriac immediately with lemon juice to prevent browning. Stir together all ingredients. Let sit an hour or overnight to soften and allow the flavors to meld.

Winter Salad

SERVES 4–6

Sweet, tender cabbage shines when you give it a dressing of really good, flavorful olive oil—that's key—and fresh, bright lemon juice. Tart pomegranates and toasty walnuts make this salad a little fancy, but in the winter I often dress cabbage pieces with just olive oil and lemon, and enjoy it that way. Be sure to toss the salad vigorously and thoroughly, to coat and flavor every single piece.

> ½ cup walnut pieces
>
> ½ head small red cabbage
>
> ½ head small green cabbage
>
> ½ cup pomegranate seeds
>
> 2–3 tablespoons very good olive oil
>
> 2–3 tablespoons freshly squeezed lemon juice
>
> kosher salt and freshly ground black pepper to taste

In a dry skillet over medium heat, toast walnuts until fragrant, about 3 minutes. Set aside. Remove core and tough outer leaves from cabbage. Place cabbage cut-side down on cutting board and make half-inch slices lengthwise and then crosswise, yielding bite-size squares. You should have about 3 cups of each kind of cabbage.

In a large serving bowl, toss cabbage with pomegranate seeds and toasted walnuts. Add olive oil and toss very well, coating everything. Add lemon juice and toss again. Add salt and pepper and toss some more. Serve immediately, or let it sit about an hour to soften cabbage and meld flavors.

Smothered Cabbage

SERVES 4

This technique I learned from Marcella Hazan's Essentials of Classic Italian Cooking *and adapted over the years. I almost always do as she recommends and serve this dish with browned meatballs. The cabbage should be fairly dry, not soupy, and has a nice, deep nutty flavor.*

> **1 tablespoon olive oil**
>
> **1 tablespoon butter**
>
> **1 white or yellow onion, halved and thinly sliced**
>
> **1 clove garlic, sliced very thinly**
>
> **1 head green cabbage, shredded**
>
> **salt and freshly ground black pepper to taste**

Heat olive oil and butter in a heavy-bottomed saucepan or Dutch oven over medium heat. Add onion and cook until soft, about 5 minutes. Add garlic and cook until fragrant, about 1 minute. Stir in cabbage (tongs are good for this, as your pan will be very full at first) and cook until wilted, about 10 minutes. Cover and reduce heat to low. Cook 45 to 60 minutes, stirring occasionally, until cabbage starts to turn golden brown. Remove lid, increase heat to medium-high, and cook until any residual liquid has evaporated, about 5 minutes. Season well with salt and pepper.

Roasted Cauliflower

SERVES 4–6

Roasting brings out the absolute best in cauliflower. In the oven, its mild nutty and peppery flavors emerge, and the slow roast turns it golden and tender. If you prefer florets, you could separate those instead of slicing the cauliflower, but I find big slices that lie flat on the baking sheet brown up rather than drying out, as florets tend to.

1 head cauliflower, cored, cut into ¾-inch slices (see head note)

1 tablespoon olive oil

½ teaspoon kosher salt

freshly ground black pepper to taste

½ cup finely grated Parmesan, optional (2 ounces)

Heat oven to 400 degrees. Arrange cauliflower on a rimmed baking sheet. Rub lightly on all sides with olive oil. Sprinkle with salt and pepper. Roast 45 minutes, until golden brown, flipping once during cooking. If using Parmesan, flip after 25 minutes, sprinkle with Parmesan, and return to oven for 20 minutes more.

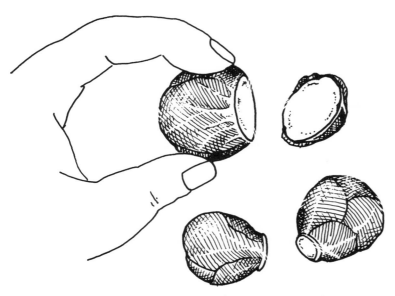

Pan-Fried Brussels Sprouts

SERVES 4

Tender, lightly sweet, and ever-so-slightly crunchy, these quickly fried brussels sprouts are best when you have young, freshly picked sprouts. They spend just enough time in the pan to take on a golden brown color and a light caramelized flavor but still taste green and cabbagey.

2 tablespoons butter or bacon grease

1 pound brussels sprouts, outer leaves removed, root trimmed, halved

2 tablespoons water

½ teaspoon salt

½ teaspoon freshly ground black pepper

2 tablespoons balsamic or other flavorful vinegar

Heat butter or bacon grease over medium-high heat in a large sauté pan wide enough to hold all the sprouts in a single layer. Add sprouts, give them quick stir to coat, and then turn them cut-side down and let cook, without stirring, 5 to 7 minutes, until golden brown on the cut side. Stir sprouts. Stir together water, salt, and pepper. Add to hot pan and cover. Steam sprouts 2 to 3 minutes. Remove lid and cook until water has evaporated. Remove from heat and stir in vinegar.

Mashed Cauliflower

SERVES 4

While cauliflower is lower in calories and carbohydrates than potatoes, this is no ersatz mashed potatoes. It's a smooth, tasty side dish in its own right. Be sure to process the cauliflower while still warm and drain it well so that it won't be watery.

> **1 head cauliflower, leaves removed, cored, cut into large florets**
>
> **2 tablespoons butter**
>
> **salt and freshly ground black pepper to taste**
>
> **½ cup crumbled blue cheese, optional**

Bring a large pot of salted water to a boil. Boil cauliflower 20 minutes, until tender. Drain well. Place cauliflower and butter in bowl of food processor and process until smooth. Season to taste. Stir in blue cheese, if using. Serve warm.

Roasted Carrots and Parsnips

SERVES 6–8

These carrots and parsnips are homey enough to eat just because and festive enough to serve with a fall dinner. The trick to sweet, delicious roasted vegetables is to lower the heat. You can roast carrots at 400 degrees and they'll be brown and crispy in about 20 minutes—but they'll still taste a little raw on the inside. I prefer to take it slow, in a 300-degree oven. I love the buttery flavor sunflower oil adds, but you can substitute olive oil if you prefer. Don't use butter, as it smokes at 250 degrees and will cloud your oven.

> **1 pound parsnips, peeled, trimmed, cut on the diagonal into 1-inch thick pieces**

1 pound carrots, peeled, trimmed, cut on the diagonal into 1-inch-thick pieces

2 teaspoons fresh thyme leaves

2 tablespoons sunflower oil

½ teaspoon kosher or sea salt

Heat oven to 300 degrees. Spread parsnips and carrots on a baking sheet and use hands to rub thyme and sunflower oil into every piece. Roast 1 hour 15 minutes, stirring every 15 to 30 minutes. Sprinkle coarse salt over top before serving.

Aunt Adelaide's Corn Bread

MAKES 16 (2-INCH) SQUARES

Aunt Adelaide spent her life on a farm in Iowa, so she knew corn and corn bread. And from her hand comes the best corn bread recipe I have ever tried. We're occasionally lucky enough to get a bag of freshly ground whole-grain cornmeal in our CSA box. Commercial cornmeal is stripped of the oily germ and the fibrous skin, so it hasn't got a lot of character or flavor. Whole-grain cornmeal is a whole different animal: rich, nutty, and flavorful, almost like buttered popcorn itself. Oh, and perishable. Keep it in the fridge.

Adelaide wasn't my aunt, but her niece, Susan, an Iowa farm girl at heart herself, has this to say about the bacon fat: "Since she was cooking for a crew of farmers who worked hard outdoors and needed lots of calories, she made bacon every morning and just kept a big vat of bacon drippings on top of the stove. Virtually everything that came from her stove or oven got a blessing of bacon drippings—including the beautiful fresh green beans right out of the garden (it actually tasted delicious!). I have substituted slightly melted butter to capture the rich, stick-to-your-ribs flavor; for those more health conscious I imagine that vegetable oil would work."

Susan adds, "Since Aunt Adelaide cooked by long-ingrained instinct, without recipes or measuring devices, it was a bit of a trick to capture any of

her recipes. As a special favor, I asked her to use measuring cup and spoons as I watched. The instructions are also my best approximation of Aunt Adelaide's rituals."

1 cup whole-grain cornmeal (see head note)

1 cup all-purpose flour

½ teaspoon salt

¼ cup sugar

4 teaspoons baking powder

1 egg

1 cup milk

4–6 tablespoons bacon drippings, melted butter, or vegetable oil

Heat oven to 375 degrees. Grease an 8-inch square pan. Mix together dry ingredients (cornmeal through baking powder) in a medium bowl. Beat together egg and milk in a small bowl and add to dry ingredients. Stir just enough to get rid of lumps of flour, but *do not beat.* Fold in fat last so that it doesn't form lumps when it hits the cool milk. Scoop into prepared pan and smooth out very gently. (Aunt Adelaide's pan was blackened by many years of use. She would spread a bit of bacon drippings in the pan and then heat it briefly in the oven before pouring in the batter to give a crisp crust.) Bake 25 to 30 minutes, until set in the center (bread bounces back after light finger pressure) and a toothpick comes out clean.

Variation: To make corn muffins, fill 8 cups of muffin tin halfway and bake at 400 degrees for 18 to 20 minutes, until set in the center and a toothpick comes out clean.

Celeriac Attack Soup

SERVES 4

For the first few years of our CSA membership, the celeriac would languish in the crisper for months, sometimes until spring. (The good news: it keeps just fine.) I tried adding it to mashed potatoes, as many people suggested, but I found it lent a metallic tang that I just didn't enjoy. I made the occasional batch of Remoulade (p. 163), but that's the sort of dish people eat by the tablespoon, not by the cupful. And then I made this soup. Now I hoard the celeriac until we have enough to make a big batch.

Butter, although you don't use much, is essential, I think, for carrying the delicate, creamy flavor. And the nutmeg—that's your secret ingredient, the one you keep to yourself when your guests are licking their spoons and wondering what that mysterious flavor is.

> 2 tablespoons butter
>
> 3 large shallots, finely chopped (about 1 cup)
>
> 3 large cloves garlic, finely grated or pressed through a garlic press
>
> 1 teaspoon salt, or to taste
>
> 3 medium celeriac bulbs, peeled and cut into ¼- to ½-inch cubes (see p. 172; about 4 cups)
>
> ¼ cup dry vermouth
>
> 3 cups broth or water
>
> ¼ teaspoon freshly grated nutmeg
>
> freshly ground black pepper to taste

Place butter and shallots in a heavy-bottomed saucepan and turn heat to medium-low. Add garlic; sprinkle with salt. Cook until shallots are soft and translucent, but not brown, about 5 minutes. Add celeriac and cook over medium heat until just barely brown, about 8 minutes. Add vermouth and cook until liquid is almost entirely absorbed, about 1 minute. Add broth or water; cover and bring to a boil. Simmer, covered, until celeriac is soft, about 15 minutes. Puree with a stick blender or in batches in a standing blender. (If you use a standing blender, fill the pitcher no more than halfway and then place a dish towel over the lid and hold it down firmly with your hand. Hot liquids in a blender can explode.) Stir in nutmeg and pepper. Makes 6 cups.

Peeling Celeriac

Celeriac bulbs are formidably ugly things: gnarled and hairy and seemingly all nooks and crannies packed with dirt. To attack your celeriac, slice off both ends and stand it up on your cutting board. You'll see a distinct inner ring in the white flesh. Line up your knife with this ring and slice downward along the outside, taking off the dirty outer layer, then rotate your bulb and keep slicing around the outside. You'll probably need to pare along the bottom to catch the stuff you missed. And you will end up discarding quite a bit of the bulb.

Your celeriac and cutting board will need a rinse at this point to get rid of loose dirt. Slice the bulb into ¼-inch-thick disks, then into ¼-inch-wide sticks, then crosswise to make cubes.

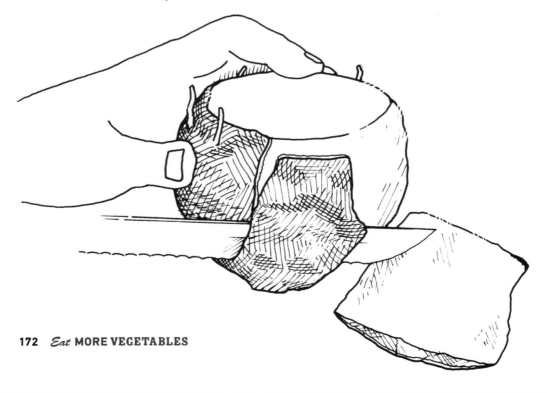

Sweet Potato Blue Cheese Soup

SERVES 4

With just enough heat, just enough tang, and just enough sweet creaminess, this is my favorite cool-weather soup. While sweet potato is often paired with foods that play up its sweetness (think marshmallows and pineapple at Thanksgiving), I prefer it with flavors that counterbalance the sweetness, like the red pepper and blue cheese here.

1 tablespoon butter

1 medium onion, chopped (about 1 cup)

¼ teaspoon salt

½ teaspoon red pepper flakes

2 medium sweet potatoes, chopped (about 4 cups)

½ cup vermouth or dry white wine

2 cups water

1 cup crème fraîche or sour cream

1 cup crumbled blue cheese, plus more for serving

Melt butter in a large saucepan. Add onion, salt, and red pepper flakes and cook over medium-low heat until very soft, about 10 minutes. Stir in sweet potatoes and vermouth or wine and raise heat to medium high. Cook until liquid is completely absorbed, 3 to 5 minutes. Add water, cover, and simmer 15 minutes, until sweet potatoes are soft. Puree carefully in batches in a blender. (Fill the pitcher no more than halfway and then place a dish towel over the lid and hold it down firmly with your hand. Hot liquids in a blender can explode. You can use a stick blender, but it won't be as silky smooth.) Stir crème fraîche and blue cheese into warm soup and serve. A little more blue cheese crumbled on top makes it even better.

Lemony Turnips and Kale

SERVES 4

Many local schools in our area invite an educator to their classrooms to talk to the kids about vegetables. Many of the kids, as he tells it, have trouble correctly identifying a potato. By the end of the lesson, after skits and art projects and plenty of practice naming vegetables in their natural state, he has the kids chanting "Close to the plant!"—meaning the less processing the better—and eager to bring a version of this recipe home to their parents. I added the lemon and nutmeg, which together make this deceptively simple dish a tasty conversion tool for vegetable—or turnip—skeptics.

> 1 tablespoon olive oil
>
> 2 cups turnip, peeled and cut into ½-inch cubes
>
> 4 cups kale, stems removed (see p. 65), cut into 1-inch pieces
>
> 2 tablespoons freshly squeezed lemon juice
>
> ¼ teaspoon kosher salt
>
> ¼ teaspoon freshly ground black pepper
>
> ¼ teaspoon freshly grated nutmeg

Heat olive oil over medium heat. Add turnips and cook 10 minutes, stirring; they'll brown a little, but mostly they should turn translucent and soft. Stir in kale, lemon juice, salt, pepper, and nutmeg. Cover, reduce heat to low, and cook 10 minutes.

Polenta with Squash

SERVES 4

Nutty, creamy, rich, and filling, polenta is a natural fit for squash. This combination should ooze out on your plate, like a very thick soup.

> 1 quart water
>
> 1 teaspoon salt
>
> 1 cup quick-cooking polenta
>
> 2 cups winter squash puree (see p. 138)
>
> ½ cup freshly grated Parmesan, plus more for serving (at least 2 ounces)

In a medium saucepan, bring water to boil and add salt. Add polenta by pouring in a thin stream, almost grain by grain, stirring constantly so it doesn't clump. Remove from heat and stir constantly until thickened, about 2 minutes. Stir in squash and cheese, vigorously beating with a wooden spoon to incorporate completely. Top with more cheese to serve.

Squash Lasagna

SERVES 8

A rich and creamy treat for the first cool nights of fall, this lasagna pairs earthy squash with an unlikely partner, a French white sauce known as Mornay, while nutmeg and sage add depth of flavor. A little goes a long way, and I've found even this small pan serves eight diners easily.

> 6 lasagna sheets
>
> 6 tablespoons (¾ stick) butter, divided
>
> 3 tablespoons flour
>
> 2 cups milk, at room temperature
>
> ½ teaspoon freshly ground black pepper

¼ teaspoon freshly grated nutmeg

2 teaspoons kosher salt, divided

1 cup grated sharp Cheddar, divided (4 ounces)

2–3 fresh sage leaves, minced

¼ onion, minced (about ⅓ cup)

2 small cloves garlic, minced (about 1 tablespoon)

2 cups winter squash puree (see p. 138)

2 tablespoons tomato paste

Heat oven to 375 degrees. Cook lasagna according to package directions. Grease an 8-inch square pan and set aside. In a medium saucepan, melt 3 tablespoons of the butter over medium heat until foaming subsides. Stir in the flour and cook, stirring, about 2 minutes, until it has a faint nutty smell but has not browned. Gradually whisk in the milk and cook, whisking, until the sauce is the consistency of heavy cream, about 5 minutes. Remove from heat and stir in pepper, nutmeg, 1 teaspoon kosher salt, and about three-quarters of the cheese. Set aside.

Melt remaining 3 tablespoons butter in a medium saucepan over medium heat. Add sage, onion, and garlic and cook until soft and translucent but not browned, about 10 minutes. Stir in squash, tomato paste, and remaining teaspoon salt. Heat through.

Spread a spoonful of sauce in the bottom of the prepared pan. Layer 2 sheets of lasagna side by side and top with about half the squash and about one-third of the sauce. Repeat. Then layer remaining 2 lasagna sheets and the last of the sauce. Sprinkle remaining cheese on top. Bake 20 minutes, until top is bubbly. Let stand at least 10 minutes before serving.

Squash Chili

SERVES 10–12

Squash skeptics—and I admit that I am one—often find that the mild-mannered cucurbit needs a little bit of kick. Or a lot. And this chili has a lot of kick. It's bone-warming and comforting and packed with nutritive goodness. The trick is to cut the squash nice and small so the texture is like chili and not like squash in sauce. Definitely use butternut squash for this recipe: it is easy to peel and cut and will hold its shape nicely.

2 tablespoons olive oil

1 medium onion, chopped

3 large cloves garlic

2 tablespoons chili powder

1 tablespoon ground cumin

1 tablespoon dried oregano

1 teaspoon ground allspice

2 dried red peppers, seeds and ribs removed, chopped

4 cups chopped plum tomatoes in their own juices
(2 [15-ounce] cans)

¼ cup dry red wine

4 pounds butternut squash, peeled and cut into ½-inch cubes

salt and pepper to taste

small bunch cilantro, chopped

Place oil, onion, garlic, and spices (chili powder through red pepper) in a large, heavy-bottomed saucepan over medium-low heat. Stirring occasionally, cook until onion is soft and translucent, about 8 to 10 minutes. Stir in tomatoes, wine, and squash. Increase heat to medium-high and bring to a low simmer. Cook until squash is soft, about 20 minutes. Season to taste. Stir in cilantro.

Pan-Fried Delicata Squash

SERVES 2

Squash aficionados love delicata squash for its thin, edible skin and its mild, floral flavor. You can bake it like any other squash, but I like the crispy edges of these slices. To serve, sprinkle with crumbled blue cheese or balsamic vinegar.

2 tablespoons olive oil

1 delicata squash, halved, seeds removed, sliced into ¼-inch-thick half moons

kosher salt and freshly ground black pepper to taste

Heat olive oil in a wide sauté pan over medium-high heat until shimmering. Working in batches, fry the squash slices until golden brown on each side, about 5 minutes total. (Try not to disturb it while it cooks, or you may tear the delicate flesh.) Season as desired and serve hot.

Grandma Lusia's Latkes

SERVES 4

The search for the perfect latke is the search for something you'll never find: the one your mom used to make. Thick or thin, cakey or dense, laced with shredded potato or smooth and fritter-like, whatever your childhood memories hold, that is *the right way to fry a latke.*

These are the latkes my husband grew up with. His mother learned the recipe from her mother during her childhood in Montreal. They tend toward the fluffy, fritter-like end of the latke scale, and the only way to achieve this texture is to separate the eggs and beat the whites. You'll appreciate this little extra bit of effort when you watch the latkes puff up in the oil and get extra crispy on the outside.

Be sure to grate the potatoes by hand. A food processor will yield long strands that make your latkes stringy. That and, as my mother-in-law quips,

"I always say you get about five drops of human blood in every batch." Latkes can be frozen and reheated in a 350-degree oven.

> **2 large or 4 medium starchy potatoes (like russets or Idahoes), peeled and grated (about 4 cups; see head note)**
>
> **2 eggs, separated**
>
> **½ medium onion, grated**
>
> **salt and pepper to taste**
>
> **2 tablespoons matzoh meal**
>
> **canola or other mildly flavored vegetable oil**
>
> **applesauce (p. 128)**
>
> **sour cream**

Wrap grated potato in a tea towel and squeeze hard to remove excess water; place potato in a large bowl. Beat egg whites to soft peaks. Stir the egg yolks, onion, salt, and pepper into the potatoes. Add matzoh and stir well. Stir a scant cup of the beaten egg whites into the potato mixture to lighten it, and then gently plop the rest of the egg whites on top of that; reaching your spatula straight down from the middle and scooping toward the outer edge, fold egg whites in lightly. Don't worry about fully incorporating them. The batter will be thin enough that you can drop it by large spoonfuls, and it will spread slightly.

Fill a heavy pan with about a quarter to a half inch of oil. Heat until a drop of water bounces on the top (about 375 degrees). Using a serving spoon, drop batter into the oil, forming patties about 3 inches across. Turn the latkes when the bottom seems firm, about 3 minutes (they should be quite crispy and dark brown). When the second side is crispy, about 2 minutes more, remove from oil. Drain on a cooling rack turned upside down over a thick layer of newspaper. Repeat with remaining batter. Serve, it goes without saying, with good applesauce and sour cream.

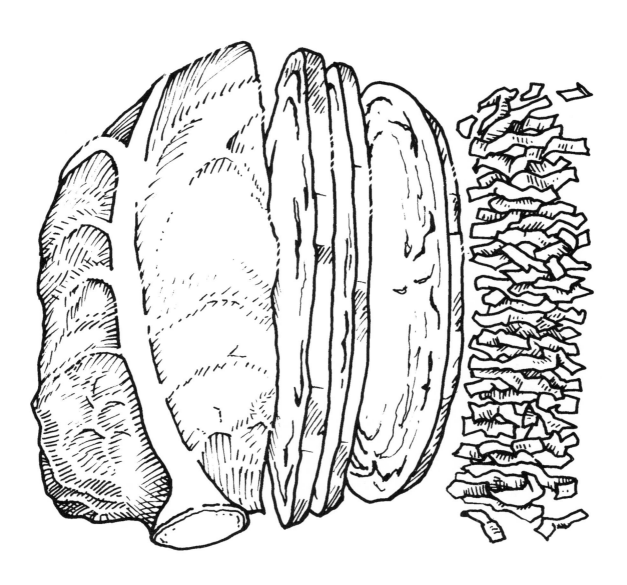

Cabbage Gratin

SERVES 6

Hearty and plain—and too often maligned—cabbage is a real favorite around our house. It carries rich flavors well and is just about the only vegetable fully at home with dairy products (which I adore). Skim milk will work, but this is a wintry treat, so I recommend whole. Gruyère's nutty flavor is ideal here, but other cheeses that melt smoothly, like fontina, would also work. This dish doesn't reheat well at all, so consider cutting the recipe in half if you're cooking for a smaller group.

> 1 (1-pound) green cabbage, quartered, cored, and shredded (see opposite; about 5–6 cups)
>
> 2 tablespoons butter
>
> 3 tablespoons flour
>
> 2 cups milk (see head note), at room temperature
>
> ½ cup grated Gruyère cheese (about 2 ounces)
>
> ½ teaspoon kosher salt
>
> ½ teaspoon freshly ground black pepper
>
> ¼ teaspoon freshly grated nutmeg

Heat oven to 375 degrees. Grease an 8-inch square baking dish. Bring a medium pot of salted water to a boil. Boil cabbage 5 minutes, strain through colander, and rinse immediately with cold water. Drain very well, squeezing lightly to remove most of the liquid.

Melt butter in medium saucepan over low heat until bubbling subsides. Stir in flour and cook, stirring, 2 minutes. Add milk all at once and stir very well to incorporate. Bring to a boil and cook 1 minute, until thickened. Remove from heat and stir in cheese. Add salt, pepper, and nutmeg. Arrange cabbage in buttered baking dish. Pour sauce over cabbage. Bake 20 minutes.

Turnip Croquettes

SERVES 4

Poor turnips. They never get invited to any parties. Even people who love turnips reserve them for homey meals instead of serving them to guests. These croquettes are like turnips decked out in party clothes. While sweet and slightly crunchy turnips are perfectly tasty without the cheese, it adds a melty, salty note.

oil

½ cup minced onion

4 cups turnip, cut into ¼-inch cubes

4 ounces cream cheese

1 egg, lightly beaten

1¼ cups matzoh meal, divided

1 teaspoon minced fresh rosemary or ¾ teaspoon dried

¼ teaspoon freshly grated nutmeg

½ teaspoon salt

¼ teaspoon freshly ground black pepper

4 ounces sharp white Cheddar, cut into ¼-inch cubes

Heat a sauté pan with a thin film of oil over medium heat. Cook onions and turnips about 5 minutes, stirring occasionally. Add a tablespoon of water, cover, and cook 10 minutes, until soft. Remove turnip mixture to a mixing bowl and mash it with the cream cheese. It will be quite chunky. Add egg, ¼ cup of the matzoh, spices, and cheese. Stir. Allow to sit for a couple of minutes to thicken.

Meanwhile, heat about quarter inch of oil in a shallow pan over medium heat. Using damp hands, roll turnip mixture into flattened golf balls. Roll in remaining cup matzoh and place gently in hot oil. Cook 3 to 4 minutes on each side, until golden brown. Remove to a paper towel–lined plate to drain. Serve warm.

Red Flannel Hash

SERVES 4–6, GENEROUSLY

When my family visits relatives in the Bay Area, we often have breakfast at a little restaurant called Rick and Ann's that has been serving "real food" to Berkeley residents since the 1980s. One of their specialties is red flannel hash. Bon Appétit published Rick and Ann's recipe in 1998, and this is my interpretation of it. I leave out the sweet potatoes and bacon and use plenty of sage and freshly ground pepper to warm up the flavor. Starchy potatoes work best with this recipe. A dollop of extra crème fraîche or sour cream for serving makes it divine.

½ pound beets, peeled, cut into ¼-inch cubes (about 1½ cups)

1½ pounds potatoes, unpeeled, cut into ¼-inch cubes (about 4 cups)

½ cup chopped onions

¼ cup crème fraîche or sour cream, plus more for serving

3 leaves fresh sage, minced

½ teaspoon kosher salt

½ teaspoon freshly ground black pepper

2 tablespoons butter, divided

Bring a pot of water to a boil. Steam beets and potatoes in a steamer basket set inside the pot for 15 minutes. Stir beets and potatoes together with next 5 ingredients (onions through pepper). Heat a large skillet over medium-high heat. Add 1 tablespoon of the butter and heat until bubbling subsides. Add half the hash mixture and press into a thick disk. Cook 2 minutes, pressing with the back of a spatula. Flip—you won't be able to flip it in one piece—and cook 2 minutes on the second side. Remove to a plate. Add remaining tablespoon of butter and repeat with second batch of hash.

Pumpkin Bread Pancakes

SERVES 8

Tender, sweet, lightly spicy pumpkin bread is a favorite in our house. Here I offer pumpkin bread in pancake form, with the same classic mix of spices. This recipe makes more pancakes than any family I know of can eat in one meal. Once I'm standing over the griddle, spooning out batter, I figure I should make more to freeze, so we always have pancakes available for weekday breakfasts. To freeze: let cool completely, stack, and wrap in a double layer of aluminum foil. As in other recipes, feel free to use any squash puree in these "pumpkin" pancakes. I'll never tell.

2 cups all-purpose flour

2 cups whole wheat flour

¼ cup sugar

4 teaspoons baking powder

1 teaspoon baking soda

1 teaspoon salt

1 tablespoon cinnamon

1 teaspoon ground cloves

1 teaspoon ground ginger

¼ teaspoon freshly grated nutmeg

3 eggs, lightly beaten

4 tablespoons (½ stick) melted butter

4 cups buttermilk

2 cups winter squash puree (see p. 138)

2 tablespoons molasses

Whisk together dry ingredients (flour through nutmeg) in a large bowl. In a separate bowl, stir together remaining ingredients (eggs through molasses). Pour wet ingredients into dry and mix together quickly, being careful not to overbeat. Heat a large griddle or skillet and gently pour batter into rounds, ¼ cup at a time, cooking 2 to 3 minutes on each side. Repeat with remaining batter.

Pumpkin Bread

MAKES 2 LOAVES

This is the fate of most of the squash and pumpkins that make it into our house. It comes from a battered notebook full of recipes I've carried with me since college. I have no memory of the provenance of the original recipes, but now I work from years of penciled-in notes and changes. It makes two loaves, so devour one now and wrap the other in two layers of aluminum foil and freeze it, for up to 3 months. Thaw at room temperature or in the refrigerator overnight.

½ cup (1 stick) butter, softened

2½ cups sugar

3 eggs

2 cups winter squash puree (see p. 138)

½ cup plain yogurt

1½ cups all-purpose flour

1½ cups whole wheat flour

2 teaspoons baking soda

1 teaspoon salt

½ teaspoon baking powder

2 teaspoons cinnamon

1 teaspoon ground cloves

1 teaspoon ground cardamom

½ teaspoon ground ginger

Heat oven to 325 degrees. Grease and flour 2 (4x8–inch) loaf pans. Beat butter and sugar until smooth and creamy. Mix together eggs, squash, and yogurt and add to butter and sugar. Mix well. Whisk together dry ingredients (flour through ginger). Add gradually to wet ingredients but do not overmix. Spread batter into prepared pans. Bake 50 to 60 minutes, until a toothpick comes out clean.

Parsnip Cake

SERVES 12

This simple, rustic cake comes together easily, like a quick bread. Parsnips' mild peppery flavor is a natural fit for the Indian-inspired spices.

Definitely take the time to shred the parsnips by hand on a box grater for nice, short shreds. Longer strings and chunks made by a food processor won't cook well in the cake. In the winter, Meyer lemon juice makes a nice substitute for the orange juice.

2 cups shredded parsnip (see head note)

½ cup orange juice

1¼ cups (2½ sticks) butter

¾ cup honey

2 eggs

1 cup all-purpose flour

1 cup whole wheat flour

½ teaspoon salt

½ teaspoon baking powder

1 teaspoon baking soda

1 teaspoon asafetida (see p. 104)

2 teaspoons ground cardamom

2 teaspoons cinnamon

1 teaspoon ground cloves

Heat oven to 350 degrees. Grease and flour a 9x13-inch pan. As you grate parsnips, mix with orange juice to prevent browning. In a small saucepan set over low heat, melt butter and stir in honey until well mixed. Let cool slightly and then stir into parsnip mixture. Beat eggs into parsnip mixture by hand. In a large bowl, whisk together dry ingredients (flour through cloves). Quickly fold in parsnip mixture, being careful not to overbeat. Pour into prepared pan. Bake 35 to 40 minutes, until a toothpick comes out clean.

ACKNOWLEDGMENTS

A kitchen is never a lonely place, but a cookbook can sometimes feel like a lonely endeavor. I want to thank the many people who made it less so. I'm fortunate to have grown up in a family of cooks. Many thanks to my parents Peter and Barbara, my sisters Laurie and Sarah, and my Aunt Nancy for testing and improving many of the recipes here. Friends old and new also lent a hand with the recipe testing and surprised me with their thorough, thoughtful, and very helpful critiques: Canice Flanagan, Jessica Griffith, Becki Howard, Becky Lien, Meleah Maynard, Eoin O'Hara, and Katrin Puusepp. Thank you, all.

My gratitude also to Michael Tortorello, who offered advice and encouragement, and to my editor Shannon Pennefeather for her sharp eye. Susan Scheckel and Sylvia Manning both shared family recipes that remain some of my favorites, as did David and Melinda Van Eeckhout of Hog's Back Farm. Of course, it is to Hog's Back Farm that I owe the original inspiration to eat more vegetables, as well as all the tasty raw materials for this book.

And it should go without saying—but they deserve to read it—that everything I cook and everything I write are inspired by love for my husband and children.

INDEX